THE
VOW-POWERED
LIFE

Also by Jan Chozen Bays

How to Train a Wild Elephant: And Other Adventures in Mindfulness

Jizo Bodhisattva: Guardian of Children, Travelers & Other Voyagers

*Mindful Eating: A Guide to Rediscovering a Healthy
and Joyful Relationship with Food*

*Mindfulness on the Go: Simple Meditation Practices
You Can Do Anywhere*

THE
VOW-POWERED
Life

A SIMPLE METHOD FOR
LIVING WITH PURPOSE

Jan Chozen Bays, MD

SHAMBHALA
Boston & London
2015

Shambhala Publications, Inc.
Horticultural Hall
300 Massachusetts Avenue
Boston, Massachusetts 02115
www.shambhala.com

9 8 7 6 5 4 3 2 1

First Edition
Printed in the United States of America

♾ This edition is printed on acid-free paper that meets
the American National Standards Institute Z39.48 Standard.
♻ This book is printed on 30% postconsumer recycled paper.
For more information please visit www.shambhala.com.

Distributed in the United States by Penguin Random House LLC
and in Canada by Random House of Canada Ltd

Designed by James D. Skatges

Library of Congress Cataloging-in-Publication Data
Names: Bays, Jan Chozen, author.
Title: The vow-powered life: a simple method for living with purpose /
Jan Chozen Bays, MD.
Description: First Edition. | Boston: Shambhala, 2016.
Identifiers: LCCN 2015013504 | ISBN 9781611801002 (alk. paper)
Subjects: LCSH: Vows (Buddhism) | Spiritual life—Buddhism.
Classification: LCC BQ4355 .B38 2016 | DDC 294.3/4446—dc23 LC record
available at http://lccn.loc.gov/2015013504

This book is dedicated to the vows of our teachers, past and present, Maezumi Roshi, Kapleau Roshi, Shōdō Harada Roshi, and Dan Brown. The power of their vows has picked us up and carried us along like a tsunami. We pass these vows on to our successors so that the immeasurable benefit of practicing the dharma will bring hope and ease to many generations as they face the unknowable and inevitable difficulties of the future.

This book is dedicated to the vows of our teachers, past and present, Maezumi Roshi, Kapleau Roshi, Shōdō Harada Roshi, and Dan Brown. The power of their vows has picked us up and carried us along like a tsunami. We pass these vows on to our successors so that the immeasurable benefit of practicing the dharma will bring hope and ease to many generations as they face the unknowable and inevitable difficulties of the future.

Contents

In Gratitude

Thank you to my husband, Hogen Bays Roshi, who has one of the most sincere life vows I have encountered and who passed on his research, experience, and deep pondering about vows to enrich this book. Although I did the writing, much of the wisdom in this book comes from him.

Thank you to all the people who tried out the exercises in classes and retreats. Thank you to David O'Neal, who became excited about vows while editing this book and gave me some good bits and pieces therein, and also to Jonathan Green, who believes in Chozen as an author more than she does herself. Uncountable thanks to my teachers and to all the fine people lit from within by vows whom I have encountered in my life, my parents first among them.

Introduction

The Power and Joy of Vows

Living by vow, silently sitting
Sixty-three years
Plum blossoms begin to bloom
The jeweled mirror reflects truth as it is.

—DAININ KATAGIRI ROSHI,
written a few weeks before his death[1]

VOWS ARE THE FORCES that weave together the fabric of your life and all of life. Without vows, without purposeful action, life would cease to exist. Vows are not a mysterious, rare, or arcane activity. Once you learn about vows, you see and hear them everywhere. They pop up in books, in magazine articles, in movies, and in ordinary conversations. Headlines often call our attention to accomplishments impelled by vows: "Woman with one leg out to conquer Everest."[2] "Six-year-old boy's dream brings water to half a million people."[3] "Muslim man saves Jewish shoppers from Islamic gunman."[4] Look around—vows are everywhere. They manifest as the book in your hands, the food in your refrigerator, the chair you are sitting on, the shelter over your head. Someone made each of these things, and that someone had to have a vow, a goal, a clear intention, in order to make it. Without vows, innovations and progress would not occur—there would have been no spearheads chipped from obsidian, no written languages, no solar panels, and there will be no future treatment for dementia.

When you begin to look at life through the lens of vows, you are touched by the dedication of human beings to not only form an aspiration to grow, change, and overcome obstacles, but also by their unselfish efforts to dedicate themselves to a larger beneficial purpose, even to an end they will not live to see manifest. Is this not the highest form of a unique human ability—the ability to form and carry out a vow? Zen masters often speak of the vows that are the fuel for their lives. Sōen Roshi,* while standing before the grave of Hakuin Zenji (a brilliant Zen master who had lived two centuries before him), was moved to compose this haiku:[5]

> Endless is my vow
> under the azure sky
> boundless autumn.

Both Katagiri Roshi and Sōen Roshi were writing about a vow without end, a vow that had been transmitted from master to disciple from the time of the Buddha down to the present, for over twenty-five hundred years of autumns. It is a primary and powerful vow, the vow to awaken to our essential nature, which is boundless and timeless, and then to help others also to awaken.

I did not understand the significance of vows until I heard my original teacher, Maezumi Roshi, speak about them several years after his death. During the almost twenty years I studied with him, he had mentioned vows many times, but somehow the real meaning and importance had escaped me. A number of years later, most of my students had never met Maezumi Roshi, and never would, so I was looking for a way to bring him alive for them. There are only a few fragments of videotape of Roshi. He was reluctant to be recorded, which was probably related to his reluctance to talk about

---

* The first time a word that might be unfamiliar appears in the text (like *Roshi* above), it will be marked with an asterisk to indicate that you can find a brief definition in the glossary.

his personal history. He felt that the dharma*, the universal truth underlying all lives, was what mattered, not the personal history of one individual.

We watched a short bit of tape that I had never seen, an interview with a person who was interested in Roshi's views about life and death. The interviewer asks him: "Christians believe in a soul that continues after this life. Do Buddhists believe in something permanent that continues after death?"

Maezumi Roshi considered the question for a moment and then replied, "No." Then he added, "Rather, we believe in the vow."

My late teacher's words struck me to the core. I instantly understood what he had been trying for many years to help me understand. I understood the power of vows.

I understood that my students and I, sitting together and watching that video, were the tangible result of my late teacher's vow. I understood that when we make a strong vow, it becomes a force that continues after we die, perhaps forever. Just as fragments of our physical energy, the calcium in our bones, and the carbon in our flesh do not disappear when we die but go on to form the bodies of new beings, so our psychic energy also continues after death and has an effect on minds and bodies well into the future. Thus the energy of a strong vow does not die with the person, but moves through time, changing as it is picked up by new people, always continuing to bear fruit.

Maezumi Roshi is a good example. He left Japan on a steamship at age twenty-six, with a one-way ticket and just a few hundred dollars in spending money. He also carried a vow: to plant the dharma so firmly in American soil that it would thrive and not die out. From the outside, his vow seemed impossible. He did not speak English, and he had no means of support beyond the small stipend paid by a Japanese-American temple. By day he served at the temple and worked as a gardener. By night he took English classes at a community college. And he sat *zazen**. Gradually, a group of Western students came to sit with him, eventually growing into a community that, after a few more years, bought a small house. Thus, as a result of Maezumi's original vow, the Zen Center of Los Angeles took shape. It grew into a complex of houses and apartment buildings that occupied almost an entire city block, housing seventy-five residents, a community clinic that was one of the first in the country to integrate Western and Eastern healing methods, and an academic institution that sponsored conferences and publications by Buddhist scholars. Out of that busy center came a lineage that includes more than one hundred authorized Zen teachers serving thousands of students in over sixty Zen centers around the world—all from what might have seemed a foolish vow, taken on with great sincerity by a determined young man.

After that experience of being struck by Maezumi Roshi's words on tape, my husband and I began to study the meaning and implication of vows. This led to the classes and retreats centered on discovering and clarifying life vows. We have found that people of all ages gain insight through the investigation of life vows, both through the process of looking at the events of their past through the discovery of their existing vows, and by assisting each other to formulate vows to guide their life in the future. This book grew out of our inquiry into the nature of vows and contains many of the exercises we did in the classes and retreats on discerning life vows.

Of course, not all vows are positive in their outcome. The result of Adolf Hitler's vow to create a "pure" Aryan race was the torture and death of six million Jews and ten million other people considered "life unworthy of life."[6] Some of the fatwas issued by terrorist leaders inspire vows to kill anyone seen as the enemy, whether civilian or military. Vows simply channel energy. We determine the direction. This book will be focused on positive vows, vows that work to relieve, not increase, the suffering of human beings and their companions on the earth.

In this book I purposely use the word *vows* instead of its synonyms. *Promises* are too easily broken. *Intentions* may be good but are too easily deflected. *Oath* has a medieval military flavor. Psychologists use the terms *goal* and *strivings* in the growing body of research that links a clear set of vows, particularly vows with a spiritual basis, with physical and emotional health and increased satisfaction in life (see the section on the psychology of vows. The words *vision* and *mission* are relevant, and I have included a chapter on the help of mission statements in formulating vows. *Deep life purpose* comes even closer. My husband, Hogen, coined the term *heart's deepest aspiration*, which is the closest to a definition for *vow* as we use it.

The word *vow* represents the actual power of a bundle of energy purposely formed, aimed, and propelled through time. This book unfolds a broader meaning of the word *vow* than you'll find in the dictionary. We look at the taking of a vow as the engine that drives human aspiration, advancement, and accomplishment. We look at each human life as a connected series of vow-led journeys, whether those journeys are short jaunts or lifelong voyages.

Some goals (you might call them "minivows") are small and last only a minute, such as the goal of finding something to drink when you are thirsty. Some of our vows are impossibly large and must be passed on to future generations, such as the vow to bring lasting peace to the world. The small, subsidiary goals are not trivial, for without drinking and eating when our body needs sustenance, we could not carry out our higher aspirations, such as bringing peace to the world.

Psychological studies on the importance of a clear sense of purpose and resultant active engagement in life are supported by research on "Blue Zones," several places around the world where people live unusually long and healthy lives. One author reports,

> Studies have linked early retirement among some workers in industrialized economies to reduced life expectancy. In Okinawa, there's none of this artificial punctuation of life. Instead, the notion of *ikigai*—"the reason for which you wake up in the morning"—suffuses people's entire adult lives. It gets centenarians out of bed and out of the easy chair to teach karate, or to guide the village spiritually, or to

pass down traditions to children. The Nicoyans in Costa Rica use the term *plan de vida* to describe a lifelong sense of purpose. As Dr. Robert Butler, the first director of the National Institute on Aging, [has said,] being able to define your life meaning adds to your life expectancy.[7]

Perhaps we should call vows "the reason you get out of bed in the morning."

WHEN IN LIFE IS IT APPROPRIATE TO WORK ON VOWS?

The work of clarifying life vows seems to be especially compelling to four groups of people: those who are just launching themselves into life after high school or college, the middle-aged, retirees, and the elderly.

Young people often are confused and hesitant about what direction to take in life. They may have dropped out of high school or college, disappointed that these institutions did not address their most urgent questions, or they may have finished college with a heavy debt burden and little chance of finding a good job. Sometimes they try holding out for a "dream job" that will enable them to put their passion to work and do what they love for a living. They are fearful that if they take a job that is less than ideal, they will be stepping on the treadmill of "owning a car to get to the job that barely pays for the car." Or they are frozen in anxiety about making a wrong choice, not aware that starting on the path is what opens the path.

Middle-aged people are drawn to work with vows when they realize abruptly that their life is half or even two-thirds over and that it is accelerating toward a now-visible finish. Retirement may provide the leisure to take a backward step, to look at a larger map of the life journey and perhaps turn off on a new freeway exit. Elderly people know that their time is now short and their life energy is fading. They want to review their life vows and their results and then see if there is something, even one thing, they can still do to benefit the world.

In the first section of this book, "About Vows," you will learn how vows work, and you will discover that you have already made and lived many vows in your life so far. We will follow the trajectory of a vow in a young physician's life, learn about the hierarchy of vows, and discover how to differentiate a vow from the means to carry out that vow.

In the second section, "Different Kinds of Vows," I will introduce three primary ways that vows are seeded and grow in our lives: by being absorbed or inherited from our family, through inspiration by human example or divine revelation, and by reaction to our experiences of suffering. Some vows are formed in childhood, when we have little understanding of how the adult world works, and those often inchoate vows can continue to operate at an unconscious level throughout our lives. If we can bring them to conscious awareness, we have the freedom to evaluate their utility and then choose whether to retain, reformulate, or discard them.

I hope that the third section, "Help in Forming Vows," does what it says. It includes some unusual sources of help, including tombstones, bucket lists, mission statements, and psychological research about the benefits of having a clear life purpose.

The fourth section, "Maintaining Vows," has suggestions for how to support your highest intentions, including some advice from one of my favorite characters in American history, Benjamin Franklin, whose creative method of reminding himself of his vows may inspire you to follow suit.

The fifth section, "The Challenges Vows Present," highlights the fact that vows are dynamic; they grow and change with us, sometimes drastically. Is it possible not to be crushed when we break a vow, or when we realize that we will not be able to complete a cherished vow in our lifetime?

The sixth section, "The Vows of Relationships," is a discussion of vows related to marriage, divorce, and, an important but seldom discussed topic, celibacy.

The seventh section, "Picked Up and Carried Along by Vows," will introduce you to inspired vows: vows birthed from other people's strong vows, vows that have a divine source, vows that are taken on amid the full realization that they are impossible, and the endless vows of the bodhisattva*.

At the end of the book, you will find an appendix with sample vows, including some of my own vows, a vows-taking ceremony, and a glossary.

Each chapter contains stories to illustrate how vows function. These stories were gathered from personal interviews, historical accounts, and biographies of famous people. Fame and vows may seem to be linked—many people have become famous, or infamous, because they had a strong vow and carried it out with wholehearted determination. When I began to interview friends, acquaintances, and even strangers, however, it was a surprise to discover that the lives of many seemingly ordinary people are guided by strong vows that they are living out with single-minded effort. I discovered that asking people about their vows (after explaining the concept) is the fastest way to turn the conversation from superficial and perfunctory to thoughtful and connecting. Try it yourself.

Speaking of trying it yourself, there are exercises scattered throughout this book. We have used many of them in our retreats on uncovering your life vows. Although useful on an individual basis, they seem to be especially enlightening and productive when contemplated and then shared in a group. The exercises, done as part of a series of classes or in a workshop or retreat setting, elicit interesting personal stories and confessions that draw the group together in the intimacy that comes from acknowledging our common struggle, our lifelong efforts to clarify and manifest our deepest life purpose.

This is my earnest wish for you. Through the power of your vows, may your life become a source of both happiness and satisfaction for you and true and lasting benefit for many others in the world.

1

ABOUT VOWS

HOW VOWS WORK

If you want to be happy, set a goal that commands your thoughts, liberates your energy, and inspires your hopes.

—ANDREW CARNEGIE

VOWS ACT LIKE a conduit for our life energy. If we do not have a clear and underlying purpose for our life, our life energy can become scattered and subject to being frittered away. Vows prevent us from reaching the end of our life and looking back with the sad question "What happened? How did I end up here?"

The underlying force that moves the world is karma. *Karma* does not mean "fate," as many people assume. It means "action." Because each action leads to an effect, you could say that cause and effect are the mechanism by which the entire world and all of its creatures are born, act, and die. Because a cause always leads to an effect, we can write this as one complete action: cause and effect. When we are confused about what action to take or what effect our actions will have, we are at the mercy of cause and effect. When we are clear about our life purpose, we take an active role in directing the chain of cause and effect.

Ordinarily we have only a vague understanding of why we act. We blunder around, driven by half-conscious motives, doing damage to ourselves and others, and then pay people like therapists, lawyers, and doctors dearly for our lack of clarity about cause and effect. Once a year, perhaps at the start of a new year, we might spend a little time reflecting on our life and formulating a few resolutions, in the hope that we will be able to lose weight, stop smoking, spend less time on the computer and more time with those we love, buy a better computer, find someone to love, begin to meditate, and read only edifying books.

Vows keep us from acting unconsciously—from becoming puppets jerked about by karmic cause and effect. They act as a compass to help us set a clear direction for our life, like our own internal GPS system (to use a modern analogy) that we can check when we feel confused or when we feel like we've lost our life direction. A vow can become a kind, patient voice inside that tells us, "Please go straight for five more miles—or five more years." It doesn't get upset if we take a wrong turn. It says, "You have wandered off course. Please return to your path to reach your desired destination." And it notes, "There is an obstacle ahead. Please plan an alternative route."

If we do not have a clear life direction, we get bumped around by other people, people who have strong agendas, often based upon their own fears, desires, and delusions. People with strong agendas may have powerful charisma but be deficient in other areas, such as ethics or financial responsibility. If we do not have the guidance of personal vows, our life becomes subject to Brownian movement, a term in physics for the random movement of molecules caused by their collision with other, faster-moving molecules. Anyone we encounter who has more energy about what they want to do in life will affect us and either carry us along or push us off in another direction, for better or worse.

For example, say a young woman starts drinking in high school, giving in to the forces of peer pressure. She gets drunk and then pregnant by someone she doesn't really like but who is very persuasive about how he "needs her." Her parents feel strongly that she should not relinquish the baby for adoption, and thus she gives up her plans to be the first in her family to go to college. She has to take a job she doesn't like in order to support her child, and so on. Everyone has examples in their life of actions they took because of a random collision with someone else who had a higher energy or a surer path in life. Some of these collisions had a good outcome; some did not.

During the years when I worked with abused children, I became interested in the fact that many adults who were raised in chaotic, abusive homes became stable, successful adults. In interviewing them I often found that what turned an abused child into a successful adult was an encounter with one adult who showed them "true north"—that is, who showed them how people *could* lead lives directed by clear intent, warm love, and simple virtue. The adult could be anyone: a foster parent, a teacher, a relative, a Big Brother or Sister. It could even be a virtual encounter with such a person, from the pages of a book, movie, or TV show. Once they had a model, these children were able to set their internal compass to north and to grow into their potential, becoming generous, happy people and good parents. It's important to be aware that you could serve, even without knowing it, to set a child or young person's internal compass correctly and provide a clear direction for his or her life. You could provide him or her with a vow.

Vows also act like a gyroscope. A gyroscope is a device that helps to maintain the upright orientation of a ship or airplane regardless of the motion of that vehicle. It stabilizes a vessel and keeps it upright in conditions that could disorient a human being, such as thick fog. When difficulties arise in our life, it is easy to become confused, frozen in indecision or depression, to lose track of where we were headed and to begin to wander aimlessly. Recollecting our vows can, like a gyroscope, help us regain our equilibrium so that we can move back to our life path again.

Recently a huge luxury liner went off course, colliding disastrously with underwater rocks, causing chaotic hours of terror for the passengers and the loss of many lives. The captain at first said that underwater radar had failed to show the rocks, but it became evident later that he had been involved in a sexual liaison that led him to ignore the truth revealed by his navigation equipment. Sexual desire is a potent force that can disorient people and knock their lives off course. For that reason every religion contains vows, commandments, or precepts to help contain sexual energy. These precepts function like dikes around a rice field. When a field is flooded with water, if there are no dikes, the water can do a lot of damage. If there are dikes, the water can nourish the new shoots of rice. Sexual energy can be very destructive or very nourishing to our life and relationships, depending upon whether it is contained by vows. In the case of the luxury liner, it's conceivable that a simple but firm vow on the part of the captain, to place the integrity of his marriage or the safety of his passengers above his temporary desire, could have averted disaster.

When we ponder what we want to do in life, we usually think, "What do *I* want to do? What will make *me* happy?" This frames our life at the center of a very small box of awareness. Vows also help us to enlarge the framework of our life so that our life energy and talents can be of real and lasting benefit to others.

"Do real and permanent good in the world"—this was the vow of a man named Andrew Carnegie.[1] His wealth enabled him to do this on a large scale, by funding the construction of three thousand public libraries, seven thousand church organs, several universities, plus an institute dedicated to studying the causes of war in order to end it and bring lasting peace to the world. He followed these principles:

> To spend the first third of one's life getting all the education one can.
> To spend the next third making all the money one can.
> To spend the last third giving it all away for worthwhile causes.

He also said, "It marks a big step in your development when you come to realize that other people can help you do a better job than you could do alone." Carnegie's life purpose was to do good in the world. He also knew that he could not carry out a vow by himself and that when other people join another person in a vow, it multiplies its effect manyfold. There are as many ways to do good in the world as there are people in the world. If we formulate vows, and if we ask for help in carrying out those vows, we will channel and amplify our individual life energy so that it becomes more likely to accomplish that lasting good.

You cannot discover your vows by thinking. Your vow lies within you. It was born into the world as you were born. You came into the world with the vow to live! You cried loudly in order to get the resources you needed to accomplish that vow. You ate, drank, slept, and smiled at your parents in order to carry out that vow. You are still eating and drinking and sleeping and smiling at people in order to carry out that vow. In the course of life, you've made and carried out many other vows, which we will explore in the exercises in the next chapter. My teacher Harada Roshi calls the life force the most basic vow. If you are reading this, you are successfully living that primary vow. Maintaining and caring for your unique life means that other vows become possible.

EXERCISE

Becoming Aware of the Vows Around You

This is a way to become aware of how vows are pervasive in our lives and how vows keep things running, like the electric current that flows through our buildings, invisible but necessary. As you go through your day, become aware of the different jobs people around you are doing. Each of their jobs represents a vow or a means of accomplishing a vow. For example, as I write this, I am flying on an airplane. The pilot has a vow (firm, I hope) to take this plane safely from Portland to Boston. The stewardess is carrying out a vow to serve the people in the plane and make them comfortable. The comedian on the in-flight movie has a vow to make people laugh. I don't know what vow underlies that purpose, maybe to become famous, or perhaps to help people take their individual predicament in life more lightly. The man next to me has a short-term vow to finish reading documents before the business meeting he's headed to. That vow might actually be the means to allow him to fulfill his larger vow to provide food and clothing for his children, to be a good parent. You could make a list like this.

PERSON/JOB	UNDERLYING VOW OR PURPOSE
Airline pilot	to fly and land the plane safely
Stewardess	to serve passengers and make them comfortable
Comedian	to entertain people and make them forget they are squished into a tiny seat in a metal box hurtling through space two miles above the earth

THE VOWS YOU'VE ALREADY MADE

On my honor, I will do my best
To do my duty to God and my country and to obey
     the Scout Law;
To help other people at all times;
To keep myself physically strong, mentally awake
     and morally straight.

—THE BOY SCOUT oath, circa 2014

From what you've read so far, you should realize that you have been making and carrying out vows all your life. Most of those vows were formed only vaguely in your mind or may even have been made unconsciously. A few, like marriage vows, were deliberately devised by you or your tradition and made in public. Some were transmitted to you, even in childhood, by adults.

Do you remember vows or promises you made in childhood? If you belonged to a club or a youth group, you likely recited oaths or promises, like the one above and the others below.

This is the Girl Scout promise.

> On my honor, I will try:
> To serve God and my country,
> To help people at all times,
> And to live by the Girl Scout Law.

> *Girl Scout Law*
>
> I will do my best to be
> honest and fair,
> friendly and helpful,
> considerate and caring,
> courageous and strong, and
> responsible for what I say and do,
> and to
> respect myself and others,
> respect authority,
> use resources wisely,
> make the world a better place, and
> be a sister to every Girl Scout.

Here is the 4-H pledge.

> I pledge my head to clearer thinking,
> My heart to greater loyalty,
> My hands to larger service,
> and my health to better living,
> for my club, my community, my country,
> and my world.

When you read these youthful vows from the perspective of adulthood, you realize that they are vows of great strength, wide in scope and intended as steady guides for earnest children, naïve about the complex problems of the adult world. And though the children who recite them may not understand them completely, making such vows at an early age may help young people begin to frame their lives in less self-centered ways and to believe that they have the ability to do good in their communities and in the world.

When you look at your life through the lens of vows, you begin to see that every accomplishment involves an intention, a kind of vow. For example, if you learned to play a musical instrument, you made an initial decision and then kept renewing your intention to develop that skill, even when practicing was tedious and playmates or a good book were calling you away. If you learned to sew and made a dress, if you practiced and finally learned to throw a bowl on a pottery wheel, if you learned how to change the oil in your car, each activity involved a small vow. If you graduated from college, you entered with a vow to finish despite long hours on weekends writing term papers or making up a missed assignment. If you raised children, you made a vow to become a good parent and renewed that vow over and over, in the face of smelly diapers, vomit on your new shirt, and uncooperative teenagers. These vows may not have been stated out loud, but they weave the fabric of every person's life. They are what keep us going and growing, despite the obstacles that inevitably arise along the way.

EXERCISE

Discovering the Vows You Have Already Made

Make a list of all the things you have accomplished so far in your life. This includes such things as the schools or classes you have attended, the skills or talents you have developed, languages learned, creative projects from making scrapbooks to building houses, relationships you maintained, children or pets cared for, and your spiritual or religious life. For each thing you list, try to discern the underlying vow. Once you start, the list may become quite long. See the examples below.

ACCOMPLISHMENTS	UNDERLYING VOW
Graduated from high school and college	to become an educated person to develop my mind
Learned sign language	to be able to communicate with deaf people to learn a new culture and way of thinking
Made statues of Jizo Bodhisattva	to make me happy to provide happiness and comfort to others
Got married	(what would you put here?)
Had children	(what would you put here?)

THE TRAJECTORY OF A VOW

There is a vitality, a life force, an energy, a quickening that is translated through you into action, and because there is only one of you in all of time, this expression is unique. And if you block it, it will never exist through any other medium and it will be lost. The world will not have it.[2]

—MARTHA GRAHAM, pioneer in modern dance

As I worked on this book, I interviewed many people about how they understood their life purpose and how their life path had unfolded to clarify and support that purpose. It was a surprisingly easy and quick way to become intimate with a person I did not know, and unexpectedly, every person I asked expressed gratitude for the opportunity to see his or her life story within the framework of vow. Here is an example from among the people I interviewed that illustrates how vows are formed and how one man was led by a vow to discover what he was "supposed to do" in life.

Peter is a thirty-six-year-old man who had just finished a residency in psychiatry at a prestigious university in New England. He said that he became a doctor because "from early on it seemed to fit my personality." His father was a physician, as were several maternal uncles, so he grew up in an atmosphere laced with medical talk, but there was no pressure on him from his family to enter medicine. Once in medical school, he decided to train as a surgeon, but he found himself talking to patients at length, an activity that puzzled or even irritated the other surgeons he worked with. He also liked the "adrenaline rush" of emergency medicine and became, by his own admission, "a bit of an adrenaline junkie," but he realized that as soon as the adrenaline faded "it would be just like any other job."

As he talked to patients in the emergency room, he realized that his real interest was in people's minds and deeper motivations, including his own. He enjoyed his time in a psychiatry rotation and chose it as his specialty. He said that surgery and psychiatry are unexpectedly similar. Both involve cutting through surface layers or appearances to see what most people do not see and to find the real source of the problems beneath. Both processes excited his curiosity about what he would find within.

When asked if he had changed during the eight, often grueling, years of his medical training, he said, "I'm unrecognizable." He attributed this noticeable change in his personality to doing his own psychotherapy and to learning meditation. He said, "I was a nice guy, very political, and people liked me, but I needed backbone. Now I can speak difficult truths, and I'm much stronger and more integrated as a person."

I asked (for reasons I will explain later) if he had encountered illness at an early age. He said that when he was two or three years old he'd had a severe attack of asthma. He reacted to the antibiotics he was given and became extremely ill. His physician could not diagnose the illness, and finally his father intervened, discovered that he had a rare infection, and "literally saved my life."

When asked how he knew what direction to take in life, he told me, that a feeling of weakness or fragility leads you to your life direction, so you can learn to cope with it and then strengthen yourself through it. He first recognized this important sense of vulnerability at age twelve, when his parents fought and divorced as he was about to enter middle school. He moved with his mother from Texas to Tennessee. In that state he entered a new culture, in which his race was a social dividing factor, but, even more important, so was his academic skill. He remembered when a friend (also African American) playfully grabbed his report card, stared at it, and said in surprise, "You are a white man trapped in a black man's body!"

He felt lonely and unstable. He picked up a book written by Benjamin Carson, a distinguished African American pediatric neurosurgeon at Johns Hopkins medical school. Carson grew up in poverty, and wrote that his illiterate mother had forced him to read books from the library. As he learned about people of great accomplishment he saw that his situation was temporary and he was in control of his own destiny.[3] As Peter read, he began to feel a sense of stability in the world. "I called it God at the time, but I knew God wasn't a man in the sky. And yet there was a strong intuition that 'it' was there." And he felt it was supporting his life.

When I asked him to frame his life vow in a few words, he said, after a few seconds, "Reducing human suffering." This young man says he loves his work and does not even think of it as work. "I think of it as universal, as being with people and applying whatever means I have among my tools to reduce their suffering. Some need medication, some psychotherapy, some a listening presence, some a hug. I don't go to work. I get paid for what I naturally do."

This story is an example of someone whose life vow was shaped by inheritance, inspiration, and reaction. He inherited the vows of the several doctors in his family. He was inspired by hearing these same men describe their work, by his father's ability to save his life, and by the example of Dr. Carson. His life work may also have been formed in reaction to his early illness and brush with death.

I have found that people who become physicians often have had an experience with illness or death in their early years, either in themselves or their family. Their choice of profession may be due to an unconscious desire to gain control over the helplessness and vulnerability they felt as they faced sickness and death at an age when they had no defenses or coping skills. Incidentally, many lawyers seem to be impelled into law after an early experience of injustice. These are clear examples of reactive vows.

Reactive vows are vows made in reaction to a difficult situation, often early in life. Children are able to see that the strategies their parents adopted in order to become happy and successful are not working, and they make a vow, often unconscious, not to be like them. A child who is neglected or abused may vow never to touch alcohol or to strike his or her own children. These kinds of vows can easily have a positive outcome, but reactive vows carry the risk of overreaction. The abused child who vows never to strike his or her own children might overreact and become a parent who cannot bear to discipline even when it's needed.

Inherited vows are those positive aspirations we take on from our family or mentors. A son who inherits his father's construction business may or may not take on his father's vows to build homes of quality and to treat subcontractors with integrity. Inherited vows are so close to us that they can be hard to see. If our family valued education, we may have taken on a vow to get an advanced degree. Once I talked to a man who was quite reactive to the notion of vows. He did not like pinning down his life purpose in words and was generally averse to the idea of taking a vow. It turned out that he was Jewish, and Jews do not name "God," because to do so frames God in human terms. Also Jews, he said, do not take vows. I teased him that he had taken an inherited vow *not* to take a vow.

Inspired vows are made in response to seeing or learning about someone we come to admire. Through another's example, we expand our view of what our own life might become. We aspire to be like them, and we might even join them in fulfilling their vow. Mahatma Gandhi vowed to practice nonviolence and to speak the truth. He said, "Non-violence and truth are inseparable and presuppose one another." "Non-violence is not a garment to be put on and off at will. Its seat is in the heart, and it must be an inseparable part of our being." "Non-violence is the first article of my faith. It is also the last article of my creed."[4] His vow inspired hundreds of thousands of people and brought an end to British rule in India. His vows stirred Martin Luther King to lead thousands more in nonviolent means of challenging and changing injustices in America.

Here is a simple example of an aspect of my own life that has been shaped by reactive, inherited, and inspired vows. My mother and grandmother were artists and art teachers. I was encouraged to be creative in childhood, and my creations were never criticized, but I was sensitive to my mother's high artistic standards. I was sure that I was not an artist—that talent had skipped a generation. I decided to become a scientist. The decision was reactive but also inspired by the stunning beauty of the world revealed by a microscope in my first biology class. Only twenty years later was I finally moved to pick up tools and hesitantly begin sculpting. But in doing so I discovered an aspiration that was inherited: to work with an artistic medium and reveal together what it seems to want to become. When I read about Enkū, a seventeenth-century Japanese sculptor who wandered all over Japan carrying out a vow to carve one hundred thousand (charming) wooden Buddha statues, I was inspired to make my own vow to make one hundred thousand statues of Jizo Bodhisattva.

These three types of vows are part of what we call *conditioning*. Often we react to a situation without realizing that there is a hidden vow at work. The next three chapters and their accompanying exercises will help you look at the types of vows that may have been directing your own life—even if you've been unaware of them. When these hidden vows are brought to light, we begin to have a choice about whether to act on them or not.

DON'T CONFUSE THE MEANS WITH THE VOW

My religion is based upon truth and non-violence. Truth is my God. Non-violence is the means of realizing Him.

—MAHATMA GANDHI[5]

When formulating their vows, people often mistake the means—the way to accomplish the vow—for the vow itself. Gandhi is remembered for demonstrating the power of nonviolent protest, but he was clear that nonviolence was a means to an end, not the goal itself. His primary vow was to know the Truth that is God.

Asking why and then asking why again is an effective way to step below the means and discover the underlying vow. Once you cannot go any further with a *why* question, you likely have arrived at the primary vow.

Here is an example of how to trace a vow down to its deepest meaning. A young boy might vow to become the highest scoring player on his baseball team. We may ask him, "Why do you want to do this?" If he's able to ponder a bit, he might come up with one of many possible answers. He might want his teammates to stop bullying him and begin admiring him. Having his teammates like him is also a means, a way of becoming safe and appreciated. He might want to impress the scouts, so he can get a scholarship for college. He might want to become adept at baseball to impress a certain girl, so she'll go out on a date with him. This also is a means.

To try to uncover his deeper life vow, we have to ask why again. Why does he want to date her? To impress his friends? Because he's heard she's "easy" and he wants to have sex for the first time? Because he truly thinks he'd like to marry her?

You see how this can continue. Why does he want to marry her? Because he's lonely? Because she's good-natured and nurturing, the opposite of his abusive mother? Because he wants to have a long, happy marriage like his grandparents had? As we move down through various motives, we arrive at his wish for a deep and lasting connection to another human being. This is a universal and fundamental desire.

Thus his primary vow, if he were guided through these successive means, might be, "To form a long-lasting, loving relationship with a suitable person." If we took it a little deeper and wider, it could be framed as, "To learn to love other people genuinely, and also myself." This is general enough to allow him to find happiness in a deep friendship, as well as in a relationship that involves exclusiveness and sex.

If his desire were to get a baseball scholarship so he could afford college, the next level down would be, "In order to become educated." If we ask why again, he might say, "To get a good job," or, "To learn about international politics," both of which are still means. As we prod him along the chain of *why* questions, we could end up anywhere, from a primary vow to start an old-age home for elderly baseball players to a vow to find a way to end world hunger. These vows might be reactive (if his grandfather, who was a semipro player, is ill and too poor to afford care) or inspired (if he was touched by a TED talk on world hunger).

I interviewed Deb, the editor in chief of our small-town newspaper. Her grandfather started the paper; her grandmother, father, and mother had worked on the paper; and now her son and daughter, the fourth generation, also work there. Deb grew up in the newspaper office and had her first piece published when she was eleven. Inspired by an engaging high school English teacher, she became editor of her high school paper; she then wrote for her college paper and worked at the family paper during summer breaks. She was hired full-time after her grandmother died of a heart attack at her desk at the newspaper. After her grandfather had a stroke, Deb and her father ran the paper together. It was an age of sexism, but Deb's father wanted people to know that she was capable and talented in her own right. Deb became the editor in chief after her father had a heart attack at his desk. He survived due to drugs whose side effects worsened preexisting retinal detachment and left him blind. Deb kept him on as an advisor.

Deb has worked full-time at the paper for almost forty years. One reason is that the newspaper provided for health care and a pension for her grandparents and father, and eventually for her own family. Her son and daughter now work at the paper. Her story clearly is one of an inherited vow, a multigenerational commitment to providing personalized community news handed down for four generations. Her story also contains themes of inspired vow (an inspirational teacher in high school), of reactive vow (to prove that a woman can run a paper), and of inherited vow—a vow underlain by feelings of family obligation, loyalty, and the desire to repay the guidance and opportunities she was given.

However, the newspaper is not the vow. It is the means. When asked why the newspaper was important, Deb said that it is a service to the community. Her entire family has been involved in many aspects of community service, from founding the local Kiwanis Club, to funding a town library, to raising money to build a public swimming pool after five children drowned in the nearby river in one year. She remembers her father tying rebar in the bottom of the hole that would become the pool. If community service is the vow, then if the newspaper folds (which she admits is likely, as retail businesses leave the town and ad revenue disappears), it doesn't have to affect her vow: she can continue to serve the community in many other ways.

However, community service itself is still not the vow. It is a high-level means. Asked what she hoped would occur in the town as a result of her service projects and the work of the newspaper, she said she hoped the town would "become/remain a close-knit, caring community." She expanded on this: "I hope it will retain a culture that is healthy in all aspects—physically, emotionally, a clean and sober, safe place where kids can grow up." She sees the newspaper as a way to tie the community together and to create that culture. She actively promotes buying locally by using the newspaper to encourage that, as a way to keep people working in the community.

Local jobs provide more opportunities for adults to volunteer and attend their children's events. This creates a watchful, warm, and supportive environment.

It is extremely important to uncover the primary vow that underlies secondary vows or the activities that we call means. If publishing the newspaper is mistaken for the vow, then if it folds, Deb will feel guilty that she has failed to keep the family business alive and has thus failed to carry out her inherited vow. However, if the primary vow—the underlying reason she has worked every day for forty years on the newspaper—is clear, she can be sad about the newspaper closing but can find other ways to support a cohesive, vibrant, caring, safe community.

There's nothing wrong with having vows that are actually means. Means can be considered minivows, or subvows. If our life circumstances change, however, and we are not able to accomplish these means, we will need to know the primary overlying vow in order to be able to change our direction and not feel as if we've failed.

For a moving example of just this shift, you might wish to see the documentary called *Fierce Grace,* about how Ram Dass carried out his life work after a serious stroke.

EXERCISES

1. Distinguishing the Means from the Vow

After you've worked with vows for a while, you develop an ear for discriminating an underlying vow from the means to accomplish that vow. Ponder and discuss which each of the below might be, means or underlying vow.

- I vow to free the world of unexploded land mines.
- I vow to be more loving and appreciative of my partner/parents.
- I vow to find peace in my own heart and spread it to others.
- I vow to build my own straw bale house.
- I vow to find a cure for multiple sclerosis.

- I vow to raise a happy, healthy child.
- I vow to learn to grow organic vegetables.
- I vow to get this congressman elected.
- I vow to protect my country from terrorists.
- I vow to write a book on _____.
- I vow to see Jesus in each person I meet.

2. Distinguishing the Vow from the Means

The best way to discern if what you have picked to do is a means rather than a vow is to ask one question: Why?

If you have begun to formulate vows, you might try the *why* test to see if you can dig down to find an underlying vow. Keep going until you feel you've hit the vow at the bottom. For example, I took a minivow today not to look at the news or Internet videos until I have spent two hours working on this book. Why?

- Because I have a deadline to meet. Why do I have a deadline?
- Because it helps me get a book done. Why do I want to get this book finished?
- Because I have a vow to write two to four more books. Why do I want to write more books? (Some days the question is, why would I be crazy enough to write another book?)
- To help people in their spiritual practice. (Getting closer.) Why do I want to help people in their spiritual practice?
- Because I have seen that spiritual practice is the best way to reduce the amount of needless suffering in the world. Aha.
- If I have a stroke and cannot write, I will need to know that the intention of writing the books is to help people in their spiritual practice. Perhaps I can still help people in their spiritual practice: by meditating or praying with them, by sending them inspiring quotes, or by just listening to and loving them.

2

DIFFERENT KINDS OF VOWS

LIFE IS THE ORIGINAL VOW

A man is ethical only when life, as such, is sacred to him, that of plants and animals as that of his fellow men, and when he devotes himself helpfully to all life that is in need of help. It is good to maintain and further life; it is bad to damage and destroy life. And this ethic, profound, universal, has the significance of a religion. It is religion.

—DR. ALBERT SCHWEITZER[1]

WHEN I ASKED my teacher Shōdō Harada Roshi about vows, he said, in his succinct way, "Life is the original vow." This became a koan* for me, something to ponder.

Life is amazingly strong. Two-thousand-year-old seeds dug from excavations at Herod's tomb in Israel were sprouted and grew into a tree. Russian scientists have regenerated plants buried for over thirty thousand years in permafrost from the Ice Age. We can see it ourselves. A barren desert turns into a flowered carpet even when rain falls briefly only every few years. A new freeway is built, and within a year there are plants pushing up through the thick asphalt along the edges. Life seems to have its own vow, to persist—and, more than persist, to create new life.

When summer days begin to shorten, the plants in our monastery garden rush to produce seeds. We clip the flowering stems off the vegetables, the broccoli flowers, the bolting lettuce. We can only hold this force back for a few weeks. Eventually even the most stunted plants put up a small pitiful stem of flowers and then seeds in the push to ensure that life continues after death.

After the atomic bomb was dropped on Nagasaki, people were told that nothing would grow, that the ground would be sterile for seventy-five years. At the Sannō Shinto Shrine, camphor trees thought to be four to five hundred years old had their branches blown off and were split and charred by the blast. Within a few months, they began to sprout new leaves, a sign that gave the defeated people hope and strength to work toward recovery.

Life is defined by growth and transformation. Our vows arise from our individual desire to grow and transform, to encourage new life to emerge from our current—and soon to be old—life.

Life is what we are. Our life is what we work to continue, as we eat, sleep, exercise, build our homes, take vitamins, obey traffic lights, and make love. We work hard to expand the boundaries of our life, to learn to walk and read, to fix a toilet, to play an instrument or do algebra, to earn enough money to travel to France or go on a meditation retreat.

All other vows depend upon this original vow, to live. The people who inspire us most are those compelled by vows that are based in nurturing life: Mother Teresa, smiling in to the eyes of the dying skeletal man she has brought indoors off the streets of Calcutta as she washes his sores; Martin Luther King, marching toward the loaded guns of southern cops in order to give life to children of color not yet born.

Dr. Albert Schweitzer's remarkable life was guided by what he later called the principle of "reverence for life." As a small child, he saw an aged, limping horse being dragged to the slaughterhouse and became acutely aware of the suffering around him. He could not understand why his evening prayers were supposed to be limited to human beings. At bedtime, after he and his mother had prayed, he secretly added a more inclusive personal prayer: "Dear God, protect and bless all beings that breathe, keep all evil from them, and let them sleep in peace."[2]

When he was eight years old, he was invited by an older boy to hunt birds with slingshots. He described being reluctant but afraid to refuse:

> So we came to a tree which was still bare, and on which the birds were singing out gaily in the morning, without any fear of us. Then stooping over like an Indian on the hunt, my companion placed a pebble in the leather of his sling and stretched it. Obeying his peremptory glance I did the same, with frightful twinges of conscience, vowing firmly that I would shoot when he did. At that very moment the church bells began to sound, mingling with the song of the birds in the sunshine. It was the warning bell that came a half-hour before the main bell. For me it was a voice from heaven. I threw the sling down, scaring the birds away, so that they were safe from my companion's sling, and fled home. And ever afterwards when the bells of Holy Week ring out amidst the leafless trees in the sunshine I remember with moving gratitude how they rang into my heart at that time the commandment: Thou shalt not kill.[3]

Schweitzer was a musical prodigy, substituting for the organist at the village church at age nine. At sixteen he was so affected by hearing a piece by Wagner that he could not concentrate at school for days; another time, he was so disturbed by the harsh sound of one organ that he wrote, "The struggle for the good organ is to me a part of the struggle for truth."[4]

At age twenty-one he conceived a plan for his life. Moved by the distress and suffering of many of his fellow students, he awoke one morning convinced that he should not accept the happiness of his life as a matter of course but should give something in return for it. He set a firm intention to spend the next ten years doing what he enjoyed, studying science, music, and art, so he could devote the rest of his life "to the direct service of humanity."[5] He said this decision brought him an inward happiness to match the outward happiness created by his happy childhood. He studied theology, but when he discovered that religious "truth" varied from age to age, he decided that the essential truth was the spirit of Jesus acting in a person's heart and in the world.

At age thirty he quit his post as principal of a theological school and applied to become a missionary in the Congo, but he was turned down because of his unorthodox theological beliefs. Much to the distress of his family and friends, he decided to study medicine in order to "put love into action instead of talking about it." He graduated after seven years and raised enough money to buy supplies and support himself as head of the Lambaréné mission hospital in tropical West Africa. He was accepted, on the condition that he not upset the missionaries there by preaching or expounding his own religious beliefs.

The hospital was remote, a fourteen-day journey by raft up the Ogooué River. It was the only hospital for five hundred miles, and patients journeyed for days to be seen, often with unusual and extreme medical conditions. From the original converted chicken coop, Dr. Schweitzer built a simple hospital of corrugated iron, with wards of logs and thatch, similar to a large native hut. He had decided to sacrifice playing the organ to carry out his vow to serve as a mission doctor, but a friend gave him a pedal piano lined with zinc to withstand the tropical elements. The piano became his consolation, and he resolved to learn to play by heart the works of Bach, Wagner, Franck, and other composers. He played during lunch breaks and on Sundays. He wrote several dozen books on diverse topics: religion, philosophy, and building organs, and published collections of organ pieces by Bach. He served at Lambaréné until his death at age ninety, except for several years when he was interned in

Germany during World War I and when he toured in Europe, giving lectures and organ concerts to raise money for the hospital. After World War II, he worked with Albert Einstein against nuclear weapons and testing, and for this work he was awarded the Nobel Peace Prize in 1952.

He described the revelation he had that resolved his many years of intense effort to find an elementary and universal worldview. "For months on end I lived in a continual state of mental excitement. I let my thought be concentrated, even through all my daily work at the hospital . . . I was wandering about in a thicket in which no path was to be found. I was leaning with all my might against an iron door which would not yield." On a slow trip upriver to see the sick wife of a missionary, he sat on the deck of a river barge, pondering this problem. "Late on the third day when, at sunset, we were making our way through a herd of hippopotamuses, there flashed on my mind, unforeseen and unsought, the phrase, 'Reverence for Life.'"[6]

The implications of this insight began to unfold in his mind. He saw that all life was sacred, that no form of life was lesser or greater in value. Humans alone were conscious of the will to live, not only in themselves, but in all other living creatures. To live in unity with other beings ended one's feeling of isolation but also revealed "the puzzling and horrible law" of being alive only at the cost of other life, and the guilt of the necessity to destroy other living beings in order to live.[7] He described rejoicing over new medicines for sleeping sickness that enabled him to stop the progress of a painful disease, but he reflected each time he saw the causative germs under the microscope that he had to sacrifice some forms of life to save others.

Dr. Schweitzer described the ethic of reverence for life as the ethic of love widened into universality. He saw that no one can exist in isolation and that our unified life means that the destinies of others are our own. Thus he concluded that each person should help develop and protect life, and in doing so would realize great happiness. "His life will become in every respect more difficult than if he lived for himself, but at the same time it will be richer, more beautiful, and happier. It will become, instead of mere living, a genuine experience of life."[8]

Schweitzer said that he found the basis and direction for his life at the moment he discovered the principle of reverence for life. This is the characteristic of a primary vow. It becomes the certain, still center of all thought and action.

Let's say you take up Schweitzer's vow: to cherish all life. There could be many subvows that serve as means for accomplishing this primary vow. These could include some of the following:

- Restoring an abandoned garden, a vacant lot, or polluted barren earth.
- Working to abolish the death penalty.
- Fostering abandoned kittens.
- Becoming a doctor, nurse, or emergency medical technician.
- Working on a suicide hotline, among the homeless, or in hospice.
- Donating to a food bank or international food relief.
- Stopping the use of pesticides in your garden. Trapping insects and mice in the home to release them outdoors.
- Caring for your own life more fully in order to be able to care for others.

EXERCISES

1. Supporting Your Own Life

Sit quietly, eyes closed. Become aware of the life force within your body, wherever you find it. It might be in the flow of breath, in the pulse of the pumping heart and circulating blood, in the warmth in your belly, in the tingle of the tips of your fingers. Feel its strength. Become aware that all the cells in your body have been working night and day, since your conception, to maintain this life force. Send them your thanks.

Ask your body/your cells, "Is there anything I can do or change in order to help support your life?"

2. Supporting the Life outside You

Sit quietly outdoors. Become aware of the life force in your surroundings. Be curious about where you might find life—beyond plants and people. Hold the awareness of the flow of life around you for ten minutes.

Ask the life around you, "Is there anything I can do or change to support your lives?"

INHERITED VOWS

My dad had me listening to Dr. King's speeches as soon as I was cognizant . . . Because my dad wanted to be a lawyer— but stopped school to support his family—he talked about [first African American Supreme Court Justice Thurgood] Marshall and King and how their partnership was essential. While Dr. King was shattering barriers Thurgood Marshall worked through the debris. Once you decide that vestiges of racism are wrong . . . there has to be a legal framework for how those changes come to life.

My dad started writing my life out in letters, when I was 9 or 10. He was writing to me about how he hoped my life would turn out—and law was a theme. I decided to (become a lawyer and) go into politics—specifically that I wanted to be mayor—when I was 13. Your parents' hopes for you really shape the trajectory of your life.

—KASIM REED, the fifty-ninth mayor of Atlanta, on the fiftieth anniversary of Martin Luther King Jr.'s most famous speech, "I Have a Dream"[9]

In childhood we are aware of what is important to our parents. Even if they do not tell us directly what their hopes are for our life, as they speak about people, we can hear the emotion in their voices, the admiration, doubt, or scorn, and through that, we can often discern their vows or aspirations. Because we want to please them, to feel the warmth of their praise, we pick up their vows. With this in mind, parents have to be careful to walk a middle way when it comes to vows, encouraging their children to fulfill their own potential but not forcing them to live out their parents' frustrated desires.

I have always wanted to learn to speak a foreign language fluently. I was able to pick up a smattering of several languages—Japanese, Korean, Spanish, and American Sign Language—and I know words for three different kinds of ice cream in Hebrew (we're talking survival in Israel in the summer). I tried to convince my children to learn a second language, but this was not their vow. If learning a second language had been one of my primary vows, I would have moved the family to Mexico for several years and put the kids in local schools, so we could all become fluent. But my primary vow manifested as the desire to study Zen, so we moved to a rough neighborhood in Los Angeles and lived at the Zen Center there, where they learned the language of awakening and how to survive in a big city.

Children may try to take on a parent's thwarted vow and then find themselves in an unhappy marriage or unsatisfying career. For example, parents might urge a daughter to marry a doctor, for financial security and status, when the girl would be happier with the man she loves who is a carpenter. Parents might work hard to establish a family business, vowing that their children will not know the privation they themselves experienced on the way up. But when the parents' dream of adding the words *and Sons* to the company letterhead comes true, the children who inherit the business might find carrying on the family vow/business a burden rather than a blessing. A woman from an extended family that has passed vast inherited wealth down over six generations told me that they all purposely train their children to take up the vow of philanthropy so that when they come of age, their inheritance is not frittered away in unfortunate ways and can become the means to benefit others.

When people become parents, the first sight of their infant, on silent black-and-white ultrasound or in squalling pink-and-wet person, may inspire a vow to love and nurture their offspring. We could call this innate bonding a form of inherited vow. The vows parents take up and the sacrifices thus entailed become especially significant when a parent has a child who is unexpectedly different. Particularly poignant examples of such adjustment can be found in Andrew Solomon's book *Far from the Tree,* which tells the stories of families who have had to reassemble their lives and reshape ordinary parental vows in circumstances where their children turned out differently than expected: when they were born with deafness, dwarfism, autism, or Down syndrome, or when they became prodigies, transsexual, or criminals.

Solomon interviewed more than three hundred families and found that many parents are transformed in a positive way, finding new purpose in life as they face the challenges of raising an unusual child. Their personal distress can turn to a passionate vow to help others in the same situation. One family founded and still supports the New York Center for Autism Charter School, even though their severely autistic son was unable to attend when he was not picked in an admission lottery. His mother observed, "I work on this school my son doesn't go to, I sponsor research that probably won't help him, and I have a think tank to design institutions where he may never receive care, because there is so little I can do to help him, and it makes me feel better to know that at least I can make some family's hope come true, the same hope I had, that never came true for us."[10]

Another mother became a more observant Jew after her son was born with Down syndrome. She said, "In the Torah, they describe building this huge tabernacle out in the wilderness, and on top of the vehicle that carries the tablets they placed two angels facing each other, because that is where God exists, between people. The day my son was born, my life became purposeful, and it has kept its purpose ever since. God exists between us. I knew that soon after he was born, but Judaism gave me a vocabulary for it."[11]

Inherited vows may have beneficial or destructive outcomes. Feuds and grudges can be nursed through many generations, flaring up into violence at any time on a slight provocation. The iconic American example is that of the famous feud between the Hatfields and McCoys, who passed their enmity on through three generations, resulting in twelve deaths.

Unfortunately, some of the most destructive inherited vows are born out of ethnic and religious prejudice that may have been handed down for centuries. A few years ago, while attending an interfaith meeting of world religious leaders in India, I encountered two examples of such inherited vows. The conference theme was forgiveness and compassion, and the Dalai Lama was a guest speaker. After the meeting, when everyone was proclaiming great affection for each other, I happened to ask a Muslim leader, a well-educated, cosmopolitan man from England, about the origin of the feud between the Sunni and Shiite sects of Islam. He became agitated, his voice rising in anger, as he described how one side had wronged the other over thirteen hundred years ago. It seemed that this inherited feud would not end soon.

I also proposed that our interfaith group could take on a concrete project to help increase interreligious understanding and lessen religiously based violence. I suggested that we could write booklets to help families whose children had married across religious lines to understand the faith tradition of their new in-laws. For example, if a Christian married a Jew, the Christian parents would get a booklet about Judaism, and vice versa. There was a sudden awkward silence, and the subject was hurriedly changed. I learned later that Orthodox Jewish parents disown their children if they marry non-Jews. This is based on the fear, perhaps well based, that the Jewish religion will die out, if not through pogroms, then through intermarriage. The underlying vow in both of these cases is not to let a specific religion or sect die out.

EXERCISE

Inherited Vows

Ponder what was important to your family, especially your parents and grandparents. Was it money, a good education, a harmonious family life, a piece of land to call their own? Think about the causes they supported, what they spent their time and money on. It might be an implicit vow, a vow they never stated out loud but that impelled their life from within. List a few people in your family. In the second column write characteristic behaviors or values they upheld. In the third, write the vow you think was under these values or behaviors. In the fourth, write the effect their vows might have had on you. See the examples from my own life below.

FAMILY MEMBER	CHARACTERISTIC BEHAVIORS / WHAT THEY VALUED	UNDERLYING VOW	EFFECT ON ME
GRANDMOTHER	Never drank alcohol / Sobriety	Temperance pledge: "Lips that touch wine will never touch mine."	I do not drink alcohol / I value a clear mind
GRANDMOTHER AND PARENTS	Good education	Learn throughout life, cultivate wisdom	I got an advanced degree

GRANDPARENTS AND PARENTS	Attended church each week	To experience God's presence, a spiritual life	I do daily meditation
GRANDMOTHER AND PARENTS	Taught Sunday school	Support others' spiritual life	I became a Zen teacher
PARENTS	Gardened and cooked	Provide food for good health	I have a big garden and good health

INSPIRED VOWS

All at once the cathedral was filled with Bach's Fugue in D Minor. It seemed to enter and possess my whole self . . . perhaps the closest I have ever come to experiencing ecstasy. It was a sort of call to action. I think I heard, in a form suitable for mortal ears, the voice of God . . . My life was taken over by a force far too strong to be resisted. . . The experience . . . put me back on track. It forced me to rethink the meaning of my life on earth.

—JANE GOODALL, primatologist[12]

Jane Goodall initially faced ridicule for her inspiration to live with wild chimpanzees in order to study their social behavior and family life. Nonetheless, she persisted for fifty-five years, becoming the only human accepted into chimpanzee society. Her work won many awards and has overturned accepted beliefs about the distinctions between humans and primates, permanently altering our ideas about "humanity."

Like Jane Goodall, some people have their life direction revealed in a striking and unambiguous way. But many people seem to plod along, heads down, seldom undergoing radical changes in their life direction. They think they will be able to be happy only when other people—and maybe the entire obstinate world—change to fit their expectations. Their hope, and thus their happiness, will never be realized. If you think about the people closest to you (a parent, partner, or grown child), how much effort would you have to exert to make them change something significant in their behavior? If you exert a lot of effort and relentless nagging, you might get them to change a small habit, like leaving ink pens in their pocket before throwing a shirt in the laundry or leaving the toilet seat up in the middle of the night. You cannot force another person to transform in a fundamental way. The only person you can transform is yourself, and even that is not easy.

I've pondered how and why people make radical changes in their lives, and it seems to occur in two ways: through sufficient suffering or through sufficient inspiration. If we suffer enough, we may become desperate enough to try another way of living in the world. I talked to a woman who had been an alcoholic for years and learned about how she had managed to become sober. The turning had occurred as she became conscious of the plight of her baby daughter, who had been born with fetal alcohol syndrome. Sometimes it's hitting bottom, being jailed, having a friend die of addiction, or even falling in love that brings about a life turning. Sometimes it's the inspiring example of an AA sponsor.

Chuck Colson, special aide to President Richard Nixon, became well known for the complete reversal in his life direction.[13] Self-described as "ruthless" and a "hatchet man," characterized by the media as "incapable of humanitarian thought," he was willing to use any means, including violence, against perceived enemies in order to reelect Nixon.[14] The consequence of that personal vow was a prison sentence for his role in the Watergate scandal. He underwent a spiritual crisis, and, inspired by the book *Mere Christianity*, by C. S. Lewis, he became an evangelical Christian. After his conversion he was disturbed by the lack of rehabilitation services in the criminal justice system, and founded the Prison Fellowship, which has become the nation's largest prison outreach program. He wrote over thirty best-selling inspirational books and initiated research showing that participation in a faith-based program called Inner Change lowered the rate of recidivism after release by two-thirds.

We enjoy conversion stories because they remind us that no one is irretrievably broken, that anyone can be inspired to change course and lead a more blessed and beneficial life. The conversion story gives us hope that, should we become deluded and hit bottom, redemption is possible.

Jizo Bodhisattva is honored in Japan as the patron saint of "lost causes," because Jizo does not see anyone as irretrievably lost or broken. Why is no one lost? Because everyone is a bud of the One Life, and thus, a bud of that which is completely Good. With proper care, that bud can grow, thrive, and experience its vibrant and continuous connection to the One Great Life. In a thousand-year-old sutra, Jizo promises that even if people have as little good as a hair, a drop of water, a grain of sand, a mote of dust, or a bit of down, that goodness can be nourished until it flourishes, and the person can "cross over" out of the land of suffering.[15]

A tiny bit of good is enough to spark a transformation. Stories of life-changing inspiration show that it could be anyone or anything that catalyzes such a change: a book, a speech, a teacher or mentor, an inner voice, a chance meeting, or an offhand comment.

Even children can be inspired to carry out a great vow, a vow that seems improbably larger than their small sphere of experience and influence. Ryan Hreljac[16] was six years old when he was startled by his first-grade teacher's explanation that many people in Africa were dying because they had no clean water. Corresponding with a pen pal in Uganda, Ryan learned that his new friend had to get up at midnight to walk four kilometers, carrying a small pot back and forth, to collect enough dirty, chocolate-colored water for his family's needs, before he left for school. Ryan was struck by the realization that he had to walk just a few steps outside his classroom to get a drink of clean water. When his teacher mentioned that it would cost just seventy dollars to dig a well, Ryan made a vow to raise money to pay for one well by doing extra chores. After four months he had earned the money, but then he learned that the actual cost of a well was two thousand dollars. Undeterred, he continued extra chores, enrolling his classmates, and eventually his entire school, in his vow, and raised enough money to build a well in his pen pal's village.

When I asked Michael Murphy, founder of the venerable re-treat center Esalen, about his life vow, he immediately said, "To bring God to earth." This vow was inspired by three words. As a twenty-year-old sophomore at Stanford University, at the end of a lecture by Frederic Spiegelberg on the ancient Indian texts the Vedas, Murphy heard the words, "Atman is Brahman" (roughly, "The fundamental nature of the [your] self is the fundamental na-ture of the entire universe"). He recalls, "A fire was lit. The doors flew open. I had an instant understanding of what it meant, that our whole being is just the budding of the cosmos, which acts through me and my works." A few months later, his vow suddenly came to him. "I got the clear message 'you have to start now' and 'burn your bridges behind you.' I quit my fraternity and moved out the next day. It was harder to quit premed and to tell my parents." Ultimately he founded the Esalen Institute. He says that everything he and the institute have accomplished over the last fifty years— the thousands of workshops, retreats, and meetings of high-level researchers, religious leaders, and politicians held at the institute, the books he has written, the extensive bibliography on meditation research he commissioned, the meditation group he leads—has all arisen from his original vow, to help people know God in them-selves and in all things.

The effect of one person's inspired vow can multiply manyfold, by inspiring other people. Kasim Reed was inspired by Martin Luther King, who was inspired by Gandhi. King and Gandhi inspired tens of thousands of people around the world to seek peace through nonvio-lent means. Michael Murphy was inspired by the Vedas, the most ancient existing religious literature, and created a sanctuary that pro-vided a nonpolitical meeting place for Soviet and US dignitaries and may have helped end the Cold War. Ryan's vow, to provide clean drinking water to those without access to it, picked up by thousands of people, became a foundation, Ryan's Well, which has provided water to almost half a million people through 329 projects in fourteen countries.

When asked about the impossibility of his vow to bring clean water and good sanitation to everyone in the world, sixteen-year-old Ryan says, "Although I am not as naïve as I was at the age of six, I know we can solve this one. I'm not saying it will be easy. Change is really hard work. It doesn't happen overnight, and it works best when everyone works together. The world is depending on us. No matter how old you are or where you come from, always remember to believe in your dreams."[17]

EXERCISES

1. Causes of Change

Have you ever made a radical change, a 180-degree turn in your life? Think of each incident and what caused it. Was it suffering or inspiration? Or other causes? I will give you examples to get started.

RADICAL CHANGE IN LIFE	CAUSE OF THAT CHANGE— SUFFERING OR INSPIRATION?
Divorce	Suffering on both sides
Started Zen practice	Inspired by my teacher's way of being
Changed college major from English to premed	Inspired by a doctor and nurse who mentored me when I worked at a hospital as a teen volunteer
Began yoga stretches	Suffering—aching body and loss of flexibility

2. Inspired Vows

Make two columns. On the left side, make a list of people you admire. On the right side, write the vows these people might inspire in you or someone else, as in the example below.

PEOPLE I ADMIRE	VOWS THEY MIGHT INSPIRE/ HAVE INSPIRED IN ME
Mother Teresa	to help those who are poor and sick
Dr. Schweitzer	to use my talents to help others
Dalai Lama	to remain compassionate in the face of persecution

REACTIVE AND OVERREACTIVE VOWS

I vowed right then and there never to lie about my age. And I never have. [My mother] demanded that we never lie to her and we were severely punished if we did. But she taught us to lie for her, to conceal her past, her marriages, her age . . . Her deceit did so much harm. It created a negative atmosphere of anger, resentment and hostility that pervaded our home. I can't help wondering if all this didn't somehow influence my choice of Sufism as a spiritual path. A Sufi is defined as a seeker of truth.

—actress ELLEN BURSTYN[18]

Reactive vows are those formed in response to something we pull away from or dislike. Sometimes that reaction can have a beneficial effect, but when the aversion is strong, it may result in an overreactive or overcompensated vow. This tends to set another reaction in motion, and the karmic swinging can go on forever if it is not tempered.

Children are more perceptive than adults realize, and they often observe that their parents' strategies for happiness did not work well. Reactive vows can ricochet through many generations. For example, a child raised by a military father who is precise, strict, authoritarian, and conservative may become a hippie. The hippie's child, tired of dirty clothes, living out of a van, and not having predictable meals, may decide to become an accountant who lives in the same house for forty years and hoards food, toilet paper, and paperclips. The accountant's child becomes a rock musician perpetually on tour; the musician's child, a buttoned-up stockbroker; and so on. It is important to identify any reactive vows we have made, so we can examine them for traces of overreaction, extra energy that can keep the ball of cause and effect bouncing back and forth generation after generation.

Here are a few stories of beneficial vows based upon reaction and also of the difficulties that can result from vows birthed out of overreaction.

A Vow of Stability in Reaction to Impermanence

From the age of three, Sonya had two close girlfriends. In their teens one got cancer, and Sonya spent three years of high school sitting in the hospital with her friend, who died at age fifteen. Through watching her friend's dying process and seeing her dead body, Sonya became intimate with impermanence. The two remaining girls went to McGill University together, where they shared a dorm room. In their second year, Sonya's roommate went on a Caribbean cruise with her mother, stepfather, and siblings. They all disappeared without a trace—no boat, no nothing. Sonya said it was very difficult because there was no closure. She lived with her dead roommate's possessions for a year as the girl's bereaved father could not bear to see anything that reminded him of his daughter.

A third loss occurred when Sonya left home to enter college. Her parents, who had had an unhappy relationship for years, divorced. They immediately jumped into other, preexisting relationships: her father, with a young woman only a few years older than Sonya, and her mother, with an equally inappropriate man. Sonya says, "I set up a whole program to be different from them—to be committed for life." She met and married a man who had a "rock-like energy, very stable." He was a student of Zen, and she began a meditation practice.

Sonya is conscious that her marriage was formed in reaction to the distress of death, disappearance, and divorce. It has been a good marriage, as good as any marriage that people work on, and the stabilizing effect of meditation has helped. She and her husband share a commitment to regular spiritual practice, to their marriage, and to their daughter.

A King's Remorse

There is a remarkable ancient document in India, inscribed indelibly in stone, that tells of a king's reactive vow. Desiring to extend his kingdom, in 261 B.C. King Asoka fought and conquered the neighboring Kalinga people. As he surveyed the carnage of the battlefield and heard the wailing of survivors, he was overcome by grief and remorse. He asked that this be recorded in stone, "One hundred fifty thousand [people] were thence carried away captive, and one hundred thousand were slain, and many times that number died. Thence arises the remorse of His Sacred Majesty for having [caused] the slaughter, death and carrying away captives . . . [It] is a matter of profound sorrow and regret." Asoka had suddenly realized that his "enemies," like himself, were faithful to their religion, loved their families, and grieved their losses. Compassion arose in his breast, and he wrote that his desire for conquest was replaced by "desires for all beings' security, self-control, peace of mind, and joyousness."[19]

King Asoka went on to establish a Buddhist polity within his sizable kingdom, forbidding cruelty to animals, animal sacrifice, and the eating of cattle, prohibiting hunting, and restricting fishing. He built veterinary clinics and hospitals, imported and cultivated medicinal herbs, and constructed roadways with rest houses and public wells at regular intervals. He had groves of fruit and shade trees planted for the benefit of travelers and established forest and wildlife preserves. Asoka encouraged his subjects to be kind, pure of heart, truthful, respectful toward elders, and generous to the poor. His twenty-three-hundred-year-old rock edicts are engraved with messages encouraging peaceful coexistence with neighboring countries and among all religions.[20]

From Coke to Carrots—the Story of a Sudden Conversion

Jeffrey Dunn was running for president of the Coca-Cola Company when he had a change of heart. He'd grown up hearing exciting "war stories" from his father about the market-share battle between Coke and Pepsi. His father was a marketing pioneer, who had helped make the soda the most powerful brand in the world. Their strategy involved linking Coke to special events in life that were suffused with positive emotions, such as a date, a holiday, or going to a ball game with your father. They also inserted Coke into "combo meals" sold at fast-food chains and into all-you-can-drink beverage bars and convenience stores. These tactics were hugely successful. By 1995 two out of three kids were drinking twenty ounces of Coca-Cola a day. Unfortunately, since that is the equivalent of fifteen teaspoons of sugar, since this was only the average consumption, and since our bodies are less aware of calories consumed in a liquid form, nutritionists and doctors began pointing to the hidden calories in soda as a significant contributor in the growing epidemic of obesity. (The company calls people who consume two or more cans a day "heavy users"—no pun intended.)

Jeffrey had worked for the company for seventeen years, becoming CEO for North and South America, marketing Coke to nine hundred million people. Looking back, he said that he loved Coke and loved being successful selling Coke. He said he simply did not think about what he was selling. In 2000 he began reading a book that had arrived unsolicited in his office. It highlighted the role of soda in the nationwide epidemic of obesity and related illnesses. Dunn also had become engaged to a woman who ate no sugar, who was concerned about preserving the Amazon rain forest, and who began to lobby him to change jobs.

In 2001 the company sent him to Brazil, a country with a booming economy and 150,000 potential heavy users. As he was touring an impoverished barrio targeted for promotion of Coke, he suddenly realized that the children he saw, like the children at home, were naïve and vulnerable to the addictive properties of the soda he was so aggressively peddling. He remembers, "A voice in my head says 'These people need a lot of things, but they don't need a Coke.' I almost threw up. From that moment forward, the fun came out of it for me."[21]

Jeffrey tried to reform the company, creating the line of Dasani bottled water and lobbying the US government not to allow Coke to be sold in public schools. In 2004 he was fired. He whispered thanks to the president who let him go and turned his formidable marketing skills to companies selling healthy snacks, like baby carrots. He described this work as "paying my karmic debt."[22]

This story is an example of a dramatic conversion, a reactive vow formed by someone who took a vow that was producing negative consequences and turned it around 180 degrees—to do good. It is an example of how a wider view can transform a self-centered vow. Jeffrey Dunn's vow changed from one of convincing people to drink what he called "sugar and fairy dust" to using the power of advertising (fairy dust) to convince people to eat healthy foods.

Vows Spawned by Hatred and Turned Around by Love

In doing research about reactive vows, I found the stories of several angry, violent men who had been active for years in the white supremacist skinhead subculture and who each had a conversion experience that turned their destructive vows around completely and set them on a beneficial life course.[23] In Zen we call these happenings "pivot points," when delusion suddenly turns to clear seeing and that clear seeing compels a change in one's life. Interestingly, all these conversions were triggered by these men's love for their own children. Here is one example.

TJ Leyden was the first person to leave the neo-Nazi movement and join a human rights organization. In his teen years, after his parents had divorced, he began hanging out on the street, venting his anger by beating up other kids. He was noticed by the neo-Nazis and became a street soldier, involved in 150 to 200 fights in a seven-year period, and later a military trainer. The vow of the movement was to create an all-white, gentile America. The means were inciting racial hatred and anti-Semitic violence.

This vow began to turn around one night when TJ was watching a TV show with Caribbean singers performing. He remembers, "My 3 year old son walked over to the TV, turned it off and said, 'Daddy, we don't watch shows with niggers.' My first impression was, 'Wow, this kid's pretty cool.' Then I started seeing something different. I started seeing my son acting like someone 10 times tougher than I was, 10 times more loyal, and I thought he'd end up actually doing something and going to prison. Or he was going to get hurt or killed. I started looking at the hypocrisy. A white guy, even if he does crystal meth and sells crack to kids, if he's a Nazi he's okay. And yet this black gentleman here, who's got a Ph.D. and is helping out white kids, he's still a 'scummy nigger.'"[24]

A year later he found the rhetoric at an Aryan Nations Congress "pathetic." He asked the man sitting next to him, "If we wake up tomorrow and the race war is over and we've won, what are we going to do next?" The man replied, "Oh, come on, T. J., you know we're going to start with hair color next, dude." On the way home, he realized, "Next it'll be you have black hair so you can't be white, or you have brown eyes so somebody in your past must have been black, or you wear glasses so you have a genetic defect." Within a year he had left the movement and joined the Task Force against Hate at the Simon Wiesenthal Center in Los Angeles (founded on Wiesenthal's vow not to allow the holocaust and its victims be forgotten, lest history be repeated).

A former skinhead recruiter, T. J. now gives speeches advocating tolerance to high school students and to military and law enforcement personnel. When asked about the personal cost of his past, he says, "[It was] my dignity. I look at myself as two people, who I am now and who I was then. I see the destruction I did to people by bringing them into the movement, the families I hurt. I ruined a lot of lives. That's the biggest thing I have to pay back. I don't forgive myself. Only my victims can forgive me."

Overreactive Vows

I lead workshops on mindful eating at our monastery. During these workshops we hear many stories of vows that are overreactive and have had difficult or harmful consequences. People who lived through the holocaust may hoard food out of a vow never to be without something to eat. They become upset if their grandchildren leave food on the plate. One woman told us about her mother, who had lived through periods of famine in Europe during World War II; she then married a GI and entered a middle-class life in America but continued to hold a fear of scarcity. She severely rationed her children's food, doing such things as marking levels on milk bottles, so her children could not "sneak" milk. She was a bad cook, so the children considered institutional school lunches "heavenly"— both in taste and because they could eat their fill.

This woman confided to us that she and her sister would save money to buy butter and a cake mix. While their mother was away, they would bake the cake, melt a half pound of butter on top, eat the entire treat by themselves, and cover their traces. She vowed that as soon as she left home, she would never go hungry. She extended her vow to others by becoming a chef in an institution—a hospital— specializing in cooking for patients who have lost their appetites. She also struggles with secret binge eating.

Here are two exercises to help you discern reactive or overreactive vows that might be present in your life.

EXERCISES

1. Identifying Your Reactive Vows

Think of things your parents or siblings did that you really disliked. Look into your life to see if you have formed any reactive vows—that is, vows *not* to do what your parents or siblings did. Look again to see if those reactive vows are well balanced or if they possibly contain elements of overreaction. Here is an example of several possible reactions to parents who forbade alcohol.

THINGS YOUR PARENTS OR SIBLINGS DID THAT YOU DISLIKED	REACTIVE VOWS?	BALANCED OR OVER-REACTIVE?	CONSEQUENCES: POSITIVE OR NEGATIVE?
Belonged to a church that forbade drinking	I drink what I like	Over-reactive	Got a DUI—Negative
	I enjoy a glass of wine a few times a week	Balanced	Positive

2. Reactive Vows to People

Make a list of people who have particular qualities or habits that you dislike. These people could be movie stars, politicians, or people in your family or workplace. On the right side, try stating a vow that might arise in reaction to these qualities. See the example.

PERSON AND QUALITIES I DO NOT LIKE	VOWS I HAVE MADE IN REACTION
Gracie Allen—nonstop talkativeness	I try to be quiet and listen more than talk
Barry—laziness, shirking responsibility	I try to always work hard and do more than my part
Aunt Mary—neat freak who yelled at her kids if one toy was out of place	I let my kids be happy making creative messes

3

HELP IN FORMING VOWS

THE TOMBSTONE TEST

My vow has always been there. When I was a teenager someone asked me the tombstone test, what I would like to be put
on my gravestone. I hadn't ever verbalized it in one line before,
but I knew what gave me joy.

—KAI, fifty-year-old itinerant street artist

I FIRST HEARD OF the tombstone test from Kai, who is a balloon
artist, street performer, and philosopher. He said that when a
friend posed this question to him, "Suddenly I realized that our
whole life is the dash on the tombstone between two dates—birth
and death. I realized that if I could write my own line on my tombstone, the summation of the dash, I could hold up that one line to
see if I'm aligned with that purpose or not, does my life match it or
not. Then I would have a chance to change course if needed. It is a
powerful method of self-guidance."

Kai was raised by an alcoholic father who was physically and
verbally abusive. His earliest memory is of dancing for some women
in a bar, at his father's request, at age six. He calls his father "the

reverse role model" but adds, "because of the way my life turned out, it was all a blessing." In school he was the class clown, a way of getting attention that landed him in the principal's office almost daily. He left home at age thirteen to live on the streets of Los Angeles, where he saw a robotic mime outside Grauman's Chinese Theatre. Kai was inspired and trained himself to stand absolutely still. He says, "At first I did it to survive, but later I realized that there was a deeper purpose."

Once he heard about the tombstone test, he began asking other people about it. "It helped me clarify my own life purpose. I'd had only a ninth-grade education and been homeless since my early teens. The first moment I realized what I was going to do for the rest of my life was when I handed a kid a balloon animal and saw the look on his face. My entertainment is seeing kids' reactions to what I do."

By age twenty his purpose had taken form. He decided that the line on his tombstone would read, "He wanted to make everyone in the world happy."

Kai cultivated the means to accomplish this vow over many years. He traded skills with other performers. He learned fire-eating from a man who wanted to learn balloon art and then juggling from someone who wanted to learn fire-eating. When a date dragged him to free introductory lessons at the Arthur Murray Dance Studios, he quickly became a dance instructor himself and began trading dance lessons for other skills. Each new skill required diligent practice. For example, it took about sixty hours of practice for him to learn the magic trick of flipping coins quickly from one finger to the next.

Kai is an avid reader, a spiritual seeker, and deeply principled. He learned clowning but stopped doing it when a mother shoved her baby in his face and the baby cried out in terror. He stopped making balloon swords after he saw a boy use one of his balloon swords to strike his sister across her knees. As he twists balloons together, he weaves in deeper teachings. When he gives a balloon to a school-aged child, he asks, "How many people did it take to bring

this balloon to you?" They make a guess, and then he says, "It takes all the people and other beings on earth, including your ancestors and mine, and even earthworms." With adults he asks, "In your body are millions of cells, each one a living being. Which one is you? All those cells are being replaced all the time, so you are a different person now than when you were born. Which one is you?" He reports that a lot of balloon artists have spiritual foundations.

Kai talks of how he learned meditation by perfecting the "live mannequin" act. He calls it a five-way meditation, involving breath (breathe so it does not show), eyes (remain open without blinking or moving no matter what passes in front of you), limbs (completely still), torso (still and balanced), and tip jar (without looking at it, you have to be constantly aware of it).

He travels continually, stopping on street corners or in restaurants to make a little money. He has gone without food so he can buy balloons, and he has used balloons to repair his old van. He smiles happily as he says, "Over the course of my career, I have learned to trust the universe to provide what I need. I don't need to worry about where things are going to come from. All my needs are taken care of. However, it often comes down to the last minute."

Kai's story illustrates many aspects of life vows. His vow to make children happy was inspired by seeing a child's smile and was thus a healthy reactive vow to his own unhappy childhood. The means to accomplish his vow have been dance, mime, magic, and balloon art. He has put a lot of effort into learning those skills and says cheerfully, "I have renounced security in society's sense." Although his itinerant lifestyle precludes intimate and ongoing friendships, it is evident that carrying out his vow has made *him* happy.

As you clarify your life vows, it can be useful to think about the tombstone test—how you would like your life to be summarized in just a few words. Would you like your family role to be engraved there? "Loving wife and mother of four." Something about your job? "A very competent administrator." Your skills? "She baked the best apple pie in the county." Your hobbies? "He kept a weed-free garden."

Your personal qualities? "He was unfailingly kind." "She was generous to everyone."

In an online discussion about the tombstone test, one woman picked this epitaph: *"She lived and loved and gave with all she had."*

EXERCISES

These exercises are fun to do in a group or with friends. Read them out loud to each other.

1. The Tombstone Test

On a piece of paper, draw a rough outline of a tombstone. Write your name, year of birth, a dash, and an imagined year of death. Underneath the dates, write a one- or two-line epitaph, something that you would like engraved on your gravestone. Here are three examples:

> He could have added fortune to fame, but caring for neither, he found happiness and honor in being helpful to the world.
>
> —GEORGE WASHINGTON CARVER,
> African American botanist and inventor

> Love one another as I have loved you.
>
> —MOTHER TERESA, quoting Jesus

> Here lies a man who knew how to enlist the service of better men than himself.
>
> —ANDREW CARNEGIE, philanthropist, written by himself

2. Advice to Yourself

Write one or two sentences of advice to your younger self. It could start with "Remember to be _____ or more _____." Here are examples:

Remember to take care of your body. It is the only one you
    have for this lifetime.
Remember to take time to stop, breathe, and open your ears
    and eyes.
Remember future generations.

Do the answers to these exercises help define an intention for
(the rest of) your life?

A BUCKET LIST

We've both been spared by a miracle. We need to think
about our passions and our purpose because life will never
be the same.

           —AMANDA NORTH's daughter, runner in the 2013
           Boston Marathon, upon finding her mother
           alive in the hospital[1]

Amanda North had always had a plan to change the world, but her
skills in the hi-tech world had continually led her along a path to
higher and more challenging positions that kept that plan on the
back burner. She said, "You . . . wake up one day and wonder, 'How
did I get here?'" She was at the finish line, waiting for her daughter
to complete the Boston Marathon, when the first bomb blast
knocked her down. Although injured, she helped others, and she is
credited with saving the life of a young woman who eventually lost
a leg.[2] Amanda says the intense experience "turned my life upside
down. It was almost like there was a rearrangement of the neural
pathways in my brain. You want to make every day count." She quit
her job and began work aligned with her primary vow, founding an
interior decorating company that supports artisans in developing
countries.

    Many people go through midlife crises. When we are young, we
think we have abundant time left in which to accomplish everything

on our long to-do list. We happily add things to the list: exotic places to visit, languages to learn, books to read, and books to write. When we reach forty or fifty, we realize that more than half the sand has drained out of our personal hourglass, and we come to terms with the fact that there are many things we will not have time to accomplish. In fact, it's time to begin throwing things overboard. If we don't, our children will end up with a half-finished boat in the garage, a few feet of an afghan begun and set aside twenty years before, a partially finished basement recreation room, boxes of unsorted slides of the Eiffel Tower at odd angles, many unopened books, desiccated art supplies, and musical instruments that were played for a few months and then abandoned.

Midlife is also a time to look back at the life vows we've been carrying and to discard, refresh, or revise them if that's needed. Realizing that we or our partner could die any time, we might invite friends and family to a renewal of marriage vows. Realizing that the possessions we accumulated as we carried out various vows will be a burden to our inheritors, we might begin paring down or giving away. I visited a man in his eighties who had been told by his doctor that his heart was failing and he had only a few weeks to live. He awoke in his wheelchair and beamed as he told us how he and his partner of sixty years had just taken a trip to the next state, where same-sex unions were allowed, and been married. He also was giving away things he had collected and loved, one by one, choosing, wrapping, and labeling carefully. He said, "This gives me great pleasure. I won't be able to use them anymore, so now someone else can enjoy them!" He died peacefully two days later.

Sometimes our assumption that we will live many more years is abruptly exploded. I once visited a young woman, a Buddhist scholar, who had aggressive liver cancer and was two weeks away from death. She lay in bed, a skeleton covered in yellow skin, with barely the strength to talk. She asked me to chant and to do a meditation with her. Afterward she said that she felt so peaceful that she was ready for death to carry her away without hesitation at that moment. As I folded and packed my priest's robes, a wisp of sadness crossed her face. "I always thought I'd have time to do [spiritual] practice later, and now there is no later."

A bucket list is one way to prioritize the things we'd like to do in the unpredictable number of years that will be given to us. Terisa Huddleston[3] made her bucket list (things to do before you "kick the bucket") at age fifty. In the course of making this list, she uncovered a life vow that picked her up and swept her off to a foreign country and a new career.

"I decided I was going to redefine my life. I called it my year of jubilee. And I made a list of 100 dreams. They ranged from a book I wanted to read to seeing the Rose Parade in Pasadena. The first 25 were easy to come up with, but by the time I reached sixty, I was really digging deep!" As she looked over the list, she realized that there were three categories: *survival,* or how to continue to live her fulfilling life in California; *creativity,* as she had begun sewing as a young child and developed a successful dressmaking business; and, as she pondered, she discovered a new aspiration to *make society better.*

Within weeks of uncovering this last vow, she found her means, or the means found her. A client asked for her assistance with a community self-help project in Peru. After years of communist rule, people there needed help learning how to run personal businesses. One of these was a training program to teach textile arts to poor women living in the barrios who were earning only ten to fifteen dollars a month. Most of the women had been abandoned by their husbands and had to leave their children alone when they went to the city to sell their scarves and sweaters. Terisa said, "I knew immediately that this was what I was meant to do."

She flew to Peru, met the women, made a few changes in their designs and colors to suit American tastes, found a wholesaler of alpaca yarn, obtained a microloan, launched an e-commerce business called Hands for Hope, and ultimately enrolled retail outlets to sell the scarves, hats, sweaters, and throws the women created. She enabled sixty women to raise their income to a middle-class level.

When one woman in the group got cancer, each of the others knit an extra item to raise money for her treatment. Terisa says, "When I started my list of 100 dreams, I had no idea where it would take me, but I'm hoping that it's just the beginning of making other women's dreams come true as well."

When we approach the end of life, we can look back and remember the life direction we aspired to at various stages in our life. We can appreciate the meanders, the forks in the road, and even the seeming detours that formed our life path. At age six I wanted to be a cowgirl, to ride a horse and lasso unsuspecting cows. At seven, I wanted to be an American Indian, to live in a longhouse and sew my clothing out of deerskin I'd chewed into softness. At age ten, the owner of a horse. At age thirteen, a particular boy's girlfriend. At age sixteen, an English major. At age eighteen, a doctor. At age twenty, a wife and teacher. At age twenty-one, a mother. At age twenty-seven, a pediatrician. At age thirty-eight, I realized that I was actually a teacher. Just give me the subject matter and a few weeks' lead time to read up, and I'd be happy to teach it.

How did I know my primary purpose in life was to teach? I was happiest when I saw that someone was confused or frustrated because they didn't understand something, and when I was able to see the source of their confusion, when I could give a little help, and when I could see understanding light up their eyes and a smile of renewed self-confidence appear on their faces. What frustrated me was bad teaching, teaching that confused people or made them feel stupid. I loved helping people experience their good minds and latent skills. The Balinese believe no one is born without musical or artistic talent. It's the job of the adults to help the children find the right medium and training to unfold their talents.

I feel the same way about people's ability to connect to the divine. Everyone has this ability, since we are all sparks of the divine, but we need tools and guidance to access what we long for.

Actually, my vow is not to teach. That's a means. My vow is to empower people, to end the particular suffering that arises when we are unable to access the true abilities of our body, heart, and mind.

EXERCISES

1. The Bucket List

Make a bucket list of at least twenty things you would like to do before you die.

Look over the list to see if these things fall into categories.

Are there any underlying vows or aspirations reflected in this list?

Take one concrete step to accomplish one of these items.

For example, when I decided to clean up some of the stuff that would burden my children when I die, I gave my working-girl clothing to an organization that helps women dress and train for job interviews, my grandmother's old mink coat to a hands-on exhibit at a local museum, my mother's unusual dolls to the Smithsonian, and my old VHS tapes to an organization that employs disabled men and women to recycle the plastic boxes.[4] I realized that this fulfilled two vows: to support and honor my family members (even those who have passed away) and to help preserve the health of the earth by keeping things out of landfills.

2. Five Years to Live

If your doctor told you that you had only five years left to live, could you think of a way to serve humanity or improve society during your remaining time? Here are some examples: teach illiterate adults to read; make quilts for abused children; make a bequest to a charity in your will.

MISSION STATEMENTS

I create a world of abundance and responsibility through creating bridges and opportunities for myself and others.

—personal mission statement of JABU MASHININI

Jabu Mashinini was a fruit and vegetable peddler on the streets of Johannesburg when he volunteered to help a missionary learn Zulu, his mother language. She hired him as a facilitator for Project TALK (Transfer of African Language Knowledge), a program to help people in South Africa—a country with eleven official languages—learn languages other than their primary language in order to foster mutual trust, bridge cultural divisions, and help bring about a more peaceful nation. He then became active with the Alternatives to Violence Project (AVP) and has brought that training to war-torn regions across Africa, to young people in high-crime areas, and to maximum security prisoners, some of whom have served as AVP facilitators after their release. Jabu Mashinini volunteers 65 percent of his time. He was awarded the international World Peace Flame, a symbol inspired by the eternal flame that burns in Mahatma Gandhi's house.[5]

The Mankind Project, a worldwide movement to empower men, emphasizes formulating a mission statement for your life. During an intensive retreat, they ask each man to answer these questions: What do you want for your future? What do you want for yourself and others? What is your unique purpose for being? What will be your action in the world to begin accomplishing that purpose?

A mission statement in this context functions like a personal vow. Action in the world is the means for accomplishing the vow, which involves undertaking sub- or minivows. Here are three more examples of the thousands of statements of "mission and action in the world" emerging from this movement.

Adam C. Personal Mission: I bring more integrity into the world by modeling accountability, mentoring the uninitiated and honoring a "second chance" concept in supporting my fellow man. Action in the World: Purchased a town home complex which now houses up to 375 formerly incarcerated men (and soon opening to women) for a 3 month-plus program preparing them to successfully re-enter society, thus reducing recidivism from nearly 60% to 20%.

Bill M. Personal Mission: I create a world of peace and justice through speaking my truth and empowering others to speak theirs. Action in the World: Providing more than 7,000 haircuts to the homeless community.

Jimmy N. Personal Mission: To create a sober and healthy world by channeling G-d's healing energy with my compassion, creativity and love. Action in the World: As an obstetrician, he has advocated for and treated 320 pregnant women in recovery and their babies.[6]

We are more familiar with mission statements in business, rather than personal, realms. Most companies have a vision or a mission statement, a succinct formulation of their purpose in the world. Mission statements guide companies, particularly as they make critical decisions. When you read a list of mission statements for large companies, you notice two recurrent themes: making a profit for shareholders and being "number one" in some domain. For example, the mission statement for PepsiCo begins, "We aspire to make PepsiCo the world's premier consumer products company focused on convenience foods and beverages. We seek to produce healthy financial rewards for investors." Publix Super Markets modestly states, "Our mission at Publix is to be the premier quality food retailer in the world." Qwest intends to be "the premier provider of full-service communications," while RadioShack has a "vision to be the most powerful one-stop shop to connect people with the wonders of modern technology." Raytheon wishes "to be recognized as the world's leading general aviation manufacturer," and Smucker's "will own and market food brands which hold the #1 market position in their respective category." Zale's mission is "to be the best fine jewelry retailer in North America," while Alcoa keeps it simple: "Our vision is to be the best company in the world."[7]

A personal vow to be "the best physicist in the world" or "to win the Nobel Prize in medicine" might make your colleagues wonder if you have narcissistic personality disorder or make them worry that you'll sneak into the lab at night and sabotage their experiments. Personal vows are not designed to bring you public recognition; they are designed to help you recognize what your life as a completely unique person is about and to begin to fulfill that potential.

At the same time, some aspects of the guidelines for developing mission statements for businesses can be helpful as we shape our individual vows. Christopher Bart writes that there are two purposes of mission statements: "to guide allocation of resources in a manner that provides consistency and focus and to inspire and motivate employees to exceptional performance—that is, to influence behavior."[8] He adds that mission statements are helpful only if they affect behavior.

This applies perfectly to life vows. Vows help us allocate our resources, time, money, and skills in a consistent manner. They inspire us to try and accomplish things beyond what we may have thought possible: learning a new language, starting a business or charity, going on a mission abroad, raising grandchildren, or sitting still and exploring our mind in a ten-day silent retreat. And, like mission statements, vows are only helpful if they change our behavior.

Two other guidelines for mission statements are relevant to our personal vows: "Keep the mission statement in front of you constantly" and "Management must say it and live it."[9]

EXERCISE

Your Mission Statement

Write a mission statement for the "business" based on your name. For example, my "business" would be "Jan Chozen Bays, Inc." I would write, "The mission of Jan Chozen Bays, Inc., is to _____."

Consider these questions:

- Who are your "customers"? That is, who in the world would you like to serve? (Hint: it doesn't have to be limited to people.)
- If your life produced more of something in the world, what would you like that "product" to be? For example, Disney Corporation wants to "make people happy," so happiness is their product.
- What would your main means of production be, to create this product? For example, if your product is better health for poor people, your means of production could be becoming a nurse, making low-cost medicine available, and so forth.
- List two values that your company respects.

Here are some key words that might be helpful: commitment, creativity, dedicated, discipline, expertise, goal, growth, joy, opportunities, positive, potential, relationships, respect, responsibility, serve, strength, support, together, unique, vision.

Share and discuss your mission statement with at least one person, ideally someone who can share his or her mission with you.

THE PSYCHOLOGY OF VOWS

Spiritual strivings tend to be related to higher levels of well-being, especially to greater purpose in life and to both marital and overall life satisfaction. Spiritual strivings appear to make a unique contribution to well-being . . . When people orient their lives around the attainment of spiritual ends, they tend to experience their lives as worthwhile, unified and meaningful.

—ROBERT EMMONS[10]

I was surprised to find that the field of psychology can offer us significant guidance as we work on clarifying our life vows. There is a sizable body of psychological research relevant to vows that psychology professor Robert Emmons has kindly summarized in his book *The Psychology of Ultimate Concerns*. Note that psychologists use the terms *personal goals* and *personal strivings* for what we call vows.

The research reveals that humans are goal-making beings, and vows are good for our health. "The possession of and progression toward important life goals are intimately tied to our long-term well-being."[11] Well-being includes a sense of purpose, a feeling of satisfaction within your life, and a conviction that your life has meaning, no matter what challenges you are currently facing. Well-being also includes enhanced physical and mental-emotional health and involvement in meaningful relationships.

In very difficult circumstances, holding clear and meaningful goals for your life can be an important factor in survival. Viktor Frankl, a psychiatrist who endured the horrors of four German concentration camps, found that people who had a "will to meaning" for their life were more likely to live through imprisonment and thrive after their release. In other words, a clear vow helped redeem their suffering and turn it to benefit for others. Frankl credits his own survival to his determination to re-create, one scribbled scrap at a time, an important manuscript that had been taken from him as he entered the camps. The manuscript was the origin of an important form of psychotherapy based on helping patients discover the deeper meaning of their lives.[12]

Certain types of life goals or vows are linked to well-being. They are *spiritual* (seeking greater intimacy with the divine), *generative* (involving creativity, giving of oneself and serving generations in the future), and those that involve *intrinsic sources of satisfaction* (self-discipline, better social skills, and self-confidence). Types of goals that do not produce well-being, and can even lower it, are those that seek *extrinsic sources of satisfaction* (power over others, material possessions, fame, physical attractiveness). Goals that are positive (actively seeking things that interest you) produce enhanced well-being, as opposed to goals that are negative (avoiding negative consequences). For example, the goal to finish a term paper or presentation can be framed in our mind in a positive way: "I want to research this topic and organize this information, so I will become a more knowledgeable person and be more skillful at my job." Or it can be framed in a negative way: "I have to get this done, so I won't get a failing grade or lose my job."

Psychologists speak of higher- and lower-level goals. Higher-level goals carry more personal value but may be too abstract for one to be able to evaluate one's own progress toward them and thus may result in stress. Lower-level goals are easier to achieve and thus less stressful, but also less meaningful. For example, it is harder to evaluate progress toward the higher-level vow to "come closer to God" compared to a lower-level vow or goal to "read the scriptures every day." A vow to "live a life of virtue" is more challenging to monitor than the intention "not to cheat at poker." The Cambridge psychologist Brian Little has termed this dilemma of undertaking meaningful versus manageable vows "the magnificent obsession versus the trivial pursuit."[13]

Research also shows that we can become distressed if we experience goals as conflicting ("devote more time to prayer and meditation and attend retreats" versus "spend more quality time with my family" or "spend more time at work perfecting my professional skills"). However, if our primary vows involve religious or spiritual growth, these higher-order vows can have a beneficial organizing effect on subordinate vows, resolving any perception of conflict and producing a greater sense of an aligned, harmonious life.

For example, if I realize that my spiritual life is not confined to the meditation hall, temple, or church pew, that all aspects of my life are infused with the sacred, then I can find fertile and felicitous ground for fulfilling my spiritual goals by bringing mindfulness to playing games on the floor with my children, or equanimity and compassion to my conversations with difficult patients or clients. Parenting becomes a sacred duty, a way to leave a beneficial legacy in the world; work becomes a calling, a way to serve God or to do my small part to reduce suffering in the world. The real testing ground of my religious life—the place to test my spiritual vows and my assortment of spiritual tools—becomes the marketplace of everyday life.

The Harvard psychologist Howard Gardner has outlined eight inherent and distinct human intelligences that humans possess in differing degrees: linguistic, logical-mathematical, spatial, musical, bodily-kinesthetic, interpersonal, intrapersonal, and naturalistic. The expression of any one of these intelligences in a certain person depends upon both genetic and environmental influences. Consider the bodily kinesthetic intelligence. Do you come from a line of (people built to be good) athletes? Did your parents play ball with you from the time you were a toddler? Consider musical intelligence. Were you born with perfect pitch? Did your parents play musical instruments and start you on lessons at age three? No matter what our genetic endowment, all the intelligences can be fostered and enhanced through practice.

Emmons argues cogently that spiritual intelligence should be added to this list. He defines *spiritual intelligence* broadly as "a realm of life concerned with ultimate purpose and meaning in life, a set of principles and ethics to live by, commitment to God or a higher power, recognition of the transcendent in daily life/ordinary experience, a selfless focus, and a set of beliefs and practices that is designed to facilitate a relationship with the transcendent."[14]

Many people set goals to develop their skills in one or more of these nine areas of competence. You could, for example (following the list of intelligences above), become fluent in a foreign language in order to become a diplomat or learn higher algebra in order to become an engineer or learn celestial navigation to be able to sail around the world or take a music composition class and write an original piece or take gymnastics classes with an aim to compete in Olympic tryouts or practice loving-kindness out of a desire to have a happier family or go into therapy to learn more about the unconscious conditioning that compels you to overeat or decide to learn about edible plants so you could survive a natural disaster. A spiritual goal might be to go to church or temple twice a week in order to become a more serene and kind person.

Emmons states that in the hierarchy of goals, the highest goals are those related to religion or spirituality—that is, to our ultimate concerns. These are the deepest questions we human beings have, questions about the ultimate purpose of our life, of all life, and about what happens to us after death. Emmons writes, "Above the line of ultimate concerns, no other concerns exist. Ultimate concern is that in which maximal value is invested, which possess the power to center one's life, and which demands total surrender. Ultimate concerns will be reflected in other [goals]."[15]

Using the examples above, the goal to learn a foreign language could be viewed as a means to a higher-order goal to become a diplomat. However, there is an even higher goal above attaining a job as a career diplomat. That superordinate goal, or primary vow, has its origin in ultimate concerns. It might be to further understanding and affection among peoples of diverse cultural backgrounds, to work toward world peace or to ensure that future generations can live free of the terrible threat of nuclear disaster. Similarly, the goal of attending religious services more regularly would be a means to a higher goal, to become a better human being. The primary spiritual vow lying above the intention to become a better person might be to emulate the saints and bodhisattvas or to live a more enlightened life or to join God in heaven when you die.

Emmons concludes: "A life that is centered around authentic spiritual goal strivings results in a life that is meaningful, valuable, and purposeful. Authentic spiritual growth involves replacing the self as the source of ultimate concern with family, community, humanity and divinity. It involves the emptying of oneself."[16]

The Practical Implications for Forming Vows

The research strongly suggests that if we want to feel satisfied on a day-to-day basis with our life, if we want to improve our health and relationships, if we want our various vows and goals to support and not conflict with each other, then the vow at the top of our list of vows should be a spiritual one. And the subordinate vows should be aligned with, support, and help actualize the primary vow. Here is an example:

1. I vow to become enlightened, however long it takes. I vow to become open to the Divine Mystery.
2. I vow to live a virtuous life, guided by the commandments or precepts for ethical living.
3. I vow to become a better parent/partner, cultivating loving-kindness, compassion, and equanimity with my children/partner.
4. Remembering the abundance in my own life, I vow to practice generosity. I will do something concrete to help others less fortunate find a better life. I will start by donating money to a college scholarship fund at an all-black college.
5. Remembering the precious gift of human life, I vow to take better care of my body so that I am able to carry out my other vows. My goals (or means) are to exercise five days a week and to eat at least one meal a day mindfully.
6. Remembering that it is more blessed to give than to receive, I vow also to help improve the health of those who do not have access to medical care. I will start by donating money to help restore eyesight to blind people in India.

4

MAINTAINING VOWS

REMINDING YOURSELF OF YOUR VOWS

It was about this time I conceived the bold and arduous project of arriving at moral perfection. I wish'd to live without committing any fault at any time; I would conquer all that either natural inclination, custom or company might lead me into. As I knew, or thought I knew, what was right and wrong, I did not see why I might not always do the one and avoid the other. But I soon found I had undertaken a task of more difficulty than I had imagined.

—BENJAMIN FRANKLIN[1]

IN 1733, at the age of twenty-seven, Benjamin Franklin undertook the vow to attain moral perfection. Although he had received only two years of formal schooling, he was an unusually intelligent, creative, inventive, civic-minded, and thoughtful man. He was a polymath, excelling at writing, printing, inventing, scientific research, politics, and diplomacy. He applied himself wholeheartedly and usually succeeded in whatever he undertook. For example, he taught himself (in one year) French, Spanish, and Latin. He was keen on chess and learned Italian by wagering chess games with a friend. The winner set a task, such as declension of Italian verbs, for the loser.

With characteristic diligence, he decided to live a fault-free life. He studied various writings on the subject and compiled a list of thirteen essential virtues. These included

- maintaining *temperance* with food and drink, not eating to dullness nor drinking to excitement;
- maintaining *silence* unless what you say will benefit others, avoiding trifling conversations;
- maintaining *order* in your physical environment, each thing in its place and time for each part of business;
- holding firm *resolution* to do what you should do without fail, performing what you resolve;
- being *frugal* and avoiding wasting resources, spending money only to do good for yourself or others;
- being *industrious* and always employed in useful pursuits, not wasting time;
- exhibiting *sincerity* and avoiding deceit, thinking innocently;
- upholding *justice* and giving benefit to everyone, injuring no one;
- maintaining *moderation* and forbearance even in response to injury, avoiding extremes;
- upholding *cleanliness* in body, clothes, and living quarters;
- exhibiting *tranquility* even in the face of unexpected accidents;
- maintaining *chastity* by using sex only for health or offspring, never to the point of harming yours or others' body, peace, or reputation; and
- being *humble*, inspired by Jesus and Socrates.

He made a notebook with a page for each virtue, and undertook a discipline of paying special attention to one virtue each week. At the end of each day, he performed a review of each of the thirteen virtues, penciling in a mark for every time he had not succeeded in upholding that quality. He planned to do four complete cycles through the thirteen virtues in one year. He was quite "surprised to find myself so much fuller of faults than I had imagined." Through diligent effort over time, he "had the satisfaction of seeing them [his faults] diminish." When he'd erased and reused those pages so often that he wore holes in them, he copied the chart on ivory slates that could be easily wiped clean.

The one virtue that gave him the most trouble was orderliness. "I found myself incorrigible with respect to Order . . . But, on the whole, tho' I ever arrived at the perfection I had been so ambitious of obtaining, but fell far short of it, yet I was, by the endeavor, a better and happier man than otherwise I should have been if I had not attempted it." At age sixty-five he ascribed the happy aspects of his life to "the joint influence of the whole mass of virtues," attributing his good health to temperance, his monetary fortune to industry and frugality, and the trust his countrymen placed in him to sincerity and justice. He advised his descendants to follow his example and thus reap the same benefits he enjoyed.[2]

Once our students have formulated life vows, we recommend that they begin each day by reciting their vows and asking for help in fulfilling them. I do this when I first sit down to meditate. I take a few minutes to settle my mind by following my breath and then silently say my vows. I don't stick to a rigid formula; the wording morphs slowly and naturally over time. It seems to set the course of the day in a beneficial direction and to catalyze the appearance of assistance in surprising forms.

You can follow Benjamin Franklin's example and do a periodic assessment of whether your vows have received some attention or been practiced. This can be done on a daily or weekly basis, depending upon the vow. This kind of review helps you notice when a vow has slipped out of your field of awareness. Even though at our Zen monastery we do retreats and classes to help formulate vows, even though we mention Jizo (the bodhisattva of great vows) in our daily chants, I find that the urgent demands of life can take over, and I lose track of the priorities set by my vows. For example, if my vow is to become compassionate and wise, and my current means to attain that vow are meditation and scripture study, then each evening I can review the day to see if I have allotted some time and life energy to at least one of those activities.

DON'T ADD FUEL TO THE INNER CRITIC

It is important to hold these exercises in examining your vows lightly. They are ways to make sure that your life hasn't become diverted from your intended direction. They are ways to notice if you haven't given time this week to one or another vow, and they provide inspiration to redirect yourself back to allocating time for the things that are important to you. It is not a way to unearth your faults or a way for the inner critical voice to scold you. Take an objective view, simply noticing if a vow needs more attention or effort. Avoid any personal conclusions about yourself. Treat yourself with patience and gentle encouragement, as you would a young child who is learning a new skill.

It is so easy for us to become distracted by trivia—such as cleaning out the spam mailbox on the computer or getting lost in a long chain of branching Internet searches. "Boy rescued from a sinkhole" becomes "Boy playing with three-legged cat" becomes "Cutest cat videos ever!" becomes an hour of wandering in the enchanted forest of the Internet. We all need some lazy time each day. You could put it in your vows under *self-care*. "I vow to take care of myself because I'm the only one of me there is. I vow to get adequate sleep, nourishing food, exercise, and to have fun each day." Don't become too serious about this. Just use the end-of-day or end-of-week check as a way to notice if you need to make adjustments in how you apportion your time, or to move certain items up to the top of your to-do list.

The exercises below suggest ways to remind yourself of your vows.

EXERCISES

1. The Ben Franklin Method

Make a grid like Franklin's in a small notebook or on an electronic notepad. Write the vows down the left-hand side, and make columns for the days of the week. Each evening, before bed, do a mental review of the day and make a check in the relevant box if you did some work on that vow that day. You might try this for a week or a month and see what you notice about each vow.

For example, if your vow is to be openhearted in all situations, you could do a very brief review at the end of the day, looking at whether your vow was tested and, if so, whether you were able to respond with warmth or kindness to the situations that arose. You could make a check mark in your notebook if you were able to maintain or manifest that intention.

Perhaps you have vows that can only be attended to once a week. If your vow is to nurture your creative potential and the primary means is a weekly pottery class, you would make a check once a week. However, a daily review might help you notice that you are actually nurturing creativity in other ways, such as cooking, carpentry, or gardening, or by looking at a museum exhibit of ancient pottery for inspiration. See the example on the following page.

2. Beginning Your Day with Vows

At the start of each day, read or recite your vows and ask for help in accomplishing them. You can say them at the beginning of morning meditation, read them before breakfast, or review them silently in the car, bus, or train on the way to work.

VOWS	MON.	TUES.	WED.	THURS.	FRI.	SAT.	SUN.
BE OPEN-HEARTED IN ALL SITUATIONS							
NURTURE MY CREATIVE POTENTIAL							
LEARN A NEW LANGUAGE							

3. The Nightly Review

This is a less formal way than Ben Franklin's method for reviewing your day in light of your vows. As mentioned above, you need to be careful not to let the inner critical voice comment on the review.

Each evening, before you go to bed, you can review your vows by considering the activities you engaged in during the day. For example, if today I spent an hour meditating, I can see that time and effort as aligned with my first vow, to become enlightened. If I also spent an hour counseling students about their Zen practice, that is time and energy aligned with my second vow, to help others to become enlightened. Since I am spending an hour today writing parts of a book on vows, I have devoted some energy to my fifth vow, to write two to seven more books that will help people with spiritual practice. As I review my day, I realize that I haven't talked to my kids or sisters in a while. Therefore I resolve to telephone or write them tomorrow, in accord with my seventh vow, to support my biological and spiritual family.

Remind yourself of your vows by writing them on a lock screen for smartphones or screen saver on your computer.

ASKING FOR HELP

Until one is committed, there is hesitancy, the chance to draw back, always ineffectiveness. Concerning all acts of initiative and creation, there is one elementary truth the ignorance of which kills countless ideas and splendid plans: that the moment one definitely commits oneself, then providence moves too. All sorts of things occur to help one that would never otherwise have occurred. A whole stream of events issues from the decision, raising in one's favor all manner of unforeseen incidents, meetings and material assistance which no man could have dreamed would have come his way.

—W. H. MURRAY, of the Scottish Himalayan expedition[3]

When we make a commitment, we must ask for help in carrying it out. There are many sources of support available, but they are waiting, inactive or invisible to us, until we ask for help. When we ask, we are admitting the truth that we cannot accomplish anything by ourselves. We have in fact never accomplished anything totally by ourselves. We did not conceive ourselves, nor did we ever create any other thing on our own. We can't even feed ourselves without a lot of help. Everything we do requires the assistance, and sometimes the lives, of countless beings, plants, animals, humans, gravity, the sun, earth, and rain.

When we ask for help, we are creating a space, like a vacuum, into which assistance can move. When we sincerely ask for help, our request can reach beings not present in this time and space. We should be aware that we are not just asking our current friends and relatives for help. We are asking a chain, a river of beings that stretches backward and forward through space and time. For example, if we make a vow to become more compassionate, we can ask all those who have embodied and taught compassion to help us. We could imagine Jesus, Mother Teresa, Saint Francis, Nelson Mandela, or the bodhisattva Kuan Yin and ask them for help. If we make a vow to become enlightened, we can imagine all the enlightened ancestors standing in a line behind us, thin and stout, men and women, young and wizened, jolly and severe. We can lean back on them when we need support. They also carried this vow; they also overcame many difficulties accomplishing it.

When our vows are unselfish, as W. H. Murray observed, "a whole stream" of help mysteriously appears. We have had so many examples of this occurring at our monastery we have begun to take it for granted. Here is a recent, almost insignificant, example. While digging in our courtyard to prepare the ground for a new Japanese garden, a young woman found a large yellowish stone with many fine layers; she thought it might be petrified wood. I told her, "I'm not sure what it is—it also could be a sedimentary rock. We need a geologist to tell us. I don't know that any of our members are interested in geology, but there's a funny thing that happens here. When you need something, it soon shows up." The next day several new people attended our Sunday meditation program. I was chatting with one young man at lunch about his confusion about what direction to take in life. I asked him, "What do you really love to do? What do you do in your free time?" He said, "Actually, I like mineralogy." I began to laugh and asked the young woman to bring the unknown stone. As soon as she put it in his hands, he said, "That's petrified wood."

We have many other examples. My dharma brother, the late Zen master John Daido Loori, told the story of a bitter winter at his old stone monastery in upstate New York when the furnace died. They had no money for repairs. The next day a man knocked on the door and asked if he could train there in exchange for work. He turned out to be a furnace repair man. Ajahn Amaro tells the story of going to live on land that had been donated as a site for a monastery in the tradition of the great Thai master Ajahn Chah. There was only one building on the property, an old farmhouse. Monks and nuns in the Thai Forest tradition live in small individual huts called *kutis*. They also observe the rules from the time of the Buddha that prohibit their handling of money and digging in the soil. They eat only donated food. Their only personal possessions are their robes, eating bowls, a sewing kit, and necessary medicine. As Ajahn Amaro was looking around the land, wondering how they could obtain kutis, a young man drove in. It turned out he had taken the wrong driveway, having intended to visit the Russian Orthodox monks on the adjoining property. When he heard about the nascent Buddhist monastery, he asked if he could help in any way. Ajahn Amaro asked him, "Do you have any particular skills?" The young man replied, "I do, but it probably won't help you. I specialize in building small sheds and outbuildings."

We have a chant at our monastery: "When this sincere request is sent forth, it is perceived and subtly answered." The word *sincere* implies that our request is heartfelt and our purpose unselfish. *Subtly* implies that we have to be alert. The response could appear in many disguised ways, such as a young man who turns up at the wrong driveway.

Often people beginning Buddhist practice are puzzled by the issue of prayer. "Since we don't have an external god in Buddhism, how can I ask for help?" The point is not whom we ask, but *that* we ask. Asking for help is an expression of humility, an admission that we cannot even negotiate the path of life, let alone carry out our vows, by ourselves. The response to our asking is not always obvious. It is seldom the response we had envisioned or hoped for. We have to be alert for where, when, and from whom the response might come. My personal rule is to be attentive and, if I hear something more than twice, to listen up! However improbable it seems, this might be the response to my request for help.

Once while I was attending a retreat in Canada, I was pondering a dilemma. I had been asked to create an online course that involved six videotaped talks, but I couldn't think of anyone who could do the filming for me. I would find myself fretting about it; then I would ask my mind to trust and let go of the worry. At dinner I overheard one of the other retreat participants mentioning that she was changing careers and becoming a professional videographer. It turned out she had done several online courses and was happy to film my course. She did such a good job that the publisher plans to use her again for other courses.

In Tibet, when you begin a spiritual practice, you "ask for the gift of influence" from the ancestors. This is called "taking refuge" in the lineage. My own experience in doing this is the comforting realization that collectively the ancestors have faced all the obstacles I will face (and more) and that they have clambered over them or walked fearlessly into them and out the other side, continuing on their Way.

Another aspect of asking for help in carrying out vows is associating with people who support, not subvert, your deepest intentions. Alcoholics and other addicts who are vowing to live a sober life take refuge, often daily, in their support groups and with their sponsors. No matter what meeting they walk into, in San Diego or Tokyo, no matter if they are dressed in Louis Vuitton or Goodwill, they can find understanding and encouragement.

The Buddha's personal attendant, Ananda, once sat down with the Buddha and his fellow monks and exclaimed with contentment, "This must be half of the blessings of our life, spiritual friendship, spiritual companionship, and spiritual camaraderie." The Buddha replied, "No, Ananda, it is the whole of the spiritual life. When a person has good people as friends, companions, and comrades, they can pursue their goal [of enlightenment]."

The Pali word for "spiritual friend" has the literal meaning of "lovely" plus "friend." A good companion is one who is pointed toward, and who helps point us toward, that which is ultimately lovely, the experience of what in Zen we call our Original Nature. This Original Nature may be expressed in running or dancing or prayer, in parenting or in service to others in a gas station or a hospice. We touch it when we forget ourselves in wholehearted activity and enter the experience of expanded self, a Self that is genuinely beautiful and true, timeless and boundless.

In truth, our life is made up of nothing but companions—everything that we call "other" is included in that category. It is these others that create our life moment by moment. Think of all the people it takes to grow, weed, pick, cook, and ship the corn to make the cornflakes in the box on our breakfast table. Now include the people who made the other ingredients in the cereal (who makes thiamine?), who designed and manufactured the box, the waxed paper liner, the ink to print the picture on the outside of the box. Now add all the people and other living beings who made it possible for you to have milk, bananas, and coffee. And that's just breakfast.

There are the people who made your sheets and pillows and toilet and water pipes and the people who keep the sewers open and pumps working, so water can flow toward you and take waste away from you. If you begin to count the supporting cast required not just to get up and eat breakfast, but to channel your life in the direction you desire, it's staggering. Your life is composed of the life energy of all these people. It flows toward, into, and through you endlessly. And you provide the same kinds of support to others: to the bare-root apple sapling vowing to grow, to the old lady vowing to cross the street to visit an ailing friend, to the store clerk vowing to support his family. When you channel all the donated energy into an active vow to help others, you are paying it back to those whose life energy gives you life, and you are paying it forward to those yet to be born.

If our friends are aligned with our goals, if we ask them to remind us of where we are headed, and especially if they will keep us company on our joint path, we are much more likely to succeed. This applies whether we are leaning on our teammates to help us get in shape for a crucial football game or asking for crowdsourcing to fund a creative project or joining a new-mom's yoga class to get back in shape. In competitive running and horse racing, pacemakers are used to keep the racer at a fast speed, but a speed they can manage for the entire race. Good path companions can keep us headed in the right direction and moving forward steadily, at the right pace, in alignment with our vows.

A path companion doesn't have to be a lifelong friend. He or she could be simply a project-long companion. When I told an acquaintance that I had signed a contract to write a book, he said that he was also working on a book. He offered, "What if I call you once a week to check up on how your writing is going, and you can nag and encourage me, too?" His cheerful calls were a big help when inspiration temporarily departed my mind.

When people begin Zen practice, they often come to me after about six months and say, "I've realized that I may have to change my friends. They want me to go barhopping, and I want to meditate." This is not a problem specific to meditation; it also could happen if you decided to devote several hours a day to practicing dance or a musical instrument. When people decide to take their life in hand and devote their energy and resources toward a particular goal, they often find that their friends do not follow along. A turning point may come as you are picked up by a vow, a point when you may need to decide to refresh your idea of who good path companions are. Ajahn Amaro describes such a turning point in his life.

Certainly, for myself, I deeply value coming across the Sangha*. I started my vague attempts at spiritual practice as a teenager; by the time I was twenty-one I was in a profound mess. It was then that I visited a branch of this monastic community in Thailand. What really impressed me there was how powerful a presence that group of people had. Simply knowing on my own that it would be a good thing for me to meditate and practice yoga, or to stop drinking and smoking did not have the same impact in helping me to break my habits, and to resist the influence of social norms. I just did not have the clarity of mind to sustain a true and honest spiritual perspective. But suddenly, being in a place where people had given up all the things that I was trying to give up, and were doing all the things that I was trying to do, it felt rather like having been lost in the wilderness and then stepping onto a bus that was heading in the right direction. At last I did not have to struggle on my own . . . To develop in the spiritual life, we need the support of companions; without that, we tend to drift or sink.[4]

EXERCISES

1. Identifying Your Ancestors

Consider: If you were to ask your "ancestors" for assistance in carrying out your vows, who would those key ancestors be? Deceased family members? Holy people and enlightened teachers? Inspiring people you have read about?

2. Asking Help from Your Ancestors

Frame a simple request or prayer, asking these ancestors for support, encouragement, and assistance. Here is an example.

I humbly ask my ancestors, biological and spiritual, and all enlightened beings through space and time to help me accomplish these vows. I am willing to give up whatever I must give up to carry out these vows (even though at times I might be frightened to do so). May all beings benefit from my vows.

3. Family and Friends

When you have a gathering of family or friends, such as a reunion or holiday get-together, ask people to tell the group about one hope or desire for their life, so that the group can affirm it and offer (at least) emotional support. Often what is revealed is a hidden aspiration. When we've done this exercise at family reunions, it has helped our family move to a deeper level of conversation and intimacy. Some of the intentions we've heard have been surprises, such as a dream of operating a quesadilla stand or working in Hawaii. Sometimes relatives have resources, monetary or others, to share. It's heartwarming when your family or friends hear and endorse your aspirations.

4. Identifying Your Supporters

Make a list of your friends. Divide the list according to who you think supports your most important life vows and who tends to distract you from them. Be thoughtful about this list. If you are a runner and your friend does not run but does help you maintain a healthy diet, he or she is actually supporting your higher goal of good health.

5. Supporting Others

Bring to mind people whom you would like to support as they carry out their life vows. Write down a few names and ways you could help them.

CEREMONIES AND VOWS

Infused with the great benevolence of Jizo Bodhisattva,
protector of all that is born from the earth,

May I welcome everything that comes toward me, with a
warm and undefended heart.
Infused with the great optimism of Jizo Bodhisattva, pro-
tector of all that is born from the earth,
May I see and nourish the seeds of awakening, in everyone
I meet.
Infused with the great determination of Jizo Bodhisattva,
protector of all that is born from the earth,
May I walk the path to Awakening, dissolving all obstruc-
tions and never turning back.
Infused with the great fearlessness of Jizo Bodhisattva, pro-
tector of all that is born from the earth,
May I know that all demons arise from ignorance, and take
refuge in the one bright Mind.
Infused with the Great Vow of Jizo Bodhisattva, protector
of all that is born from the earth,
May I gladly enter every hell realm, guiding myself and
everyone to liberation.

—from a chant at Great Vow Monastery

Vows are often made in a ceremony, and ceremonies often contain
vows. At the monastery our daily life is interwoven with ceremonies. We keep what the Catholics call the "liturgy of the hours,"
chanting services four times a day. Over the course of decades, I've
had every reaction to these services. Some days I enjoy the pag-
eantry; some days I'm distracted or impatient for them to end, and
other days I'm transported by them to another realm. I've given up
thinking I should have a particular reaction or feeling. I just try to
participate in all our ceremonies wholeheartedly.

Ceremonies help people make important commitments: to
marriage, to raising a child, to a life guided by sacred teachings. In
Zen practice there is a ceremony known as *jukai*, the taking of the
precepts, which are ethical guidelines similar to the Ten Commandments. This ceremony marks a transition from an unconscious
journey to an active undertaking, a life in which we live with vows

as a guide to help us create the least amount of suffering and the greatest amount of happiness and ease for ourselves and others. The precepts are similar to those taught by all major religions: to cherish all life and avoid killing, to respect the belongings of others and not steal, to be respectful with sexual energy and not misuse it, to be truthful and not lie, to keep the mind clear and not become intoxicated, to be generous and not greedy, and to be kind and not gossip about others' faults and errors.

To vow to commit to a relationship or to uphold the precepts, out loud, in a public ceremony, adds weight to these commitments and acknowledges the fact that they are a task too large to be done through one's own power alone. Through such public acknowledgments, we are admitting that we need the support of others, and we are asking for their discerning eye and gentle guidance should we falter. When we make a sincere vow, the resources we need to carry out that vow begin to gather and move toward us.

Ceremonies pull the energy of a group into a common purpose. We had trouble retaining board members for our organization until we learned (through an interfaith institute) something important—to create meetings that are supported by the framework of a ceremony or religious service. We begin board meetings with a few moments of silence. We intersperse committee reports with short readings from the sacred literature. At the end of each meeting, we chant together. We might have disagreed about how to approach certain items on the agenda, but when we end the meeting with a chant, it draws the group together in harmony and reaffirms our connections and common purpose.

Ceremonies help keep ancient traditions alive and thereby keep the vow energy of the ancient holy men and women alive, so it will continue to be available in the future. Every time someone reads aloud from the Torah, recites the Lord's Prayer, blesses a Native American hogan with corn pollen, chants *kirtan* (Hindu devotional chanting), or sits in the meditation posture of the Buddha, the embers of the past flare up, radiating light and giving warmth in the

Shrine of Vows, Great Vow Zen Monastery.
© Nicole Gallagher

present. The day-to-day activity of our bodies is the exact means by which that sacred energy flows out, to give benefit to us now and to generations in the future.

In China and Japan, it is common for people to buy a token and dedicate it at a temple when they make a vow. It might be a piece of paper tied to a sacred tree or a small wooden plaque on which the promise is written, to be left with many others at a shrine. A resonant recent custom one sees even in America and Europe now is to buy a padlock and fasten it to a chain-link fence. Often these padlock pledges express the hope to pass a certain exam or to love a certain person. People attached so many of these vow locks to a fence at one temple in Japan that the huge gate posts collapsed under the weight.

At the monastery we have built a Shrine of Vows, an open structure surrounded by a fence. Once people have clarified their vows, they can paint them on a stone or ceramic plaque, place them at the shrine, say their vow out loud, and ring a bell. Visitors have commented, "It's lovely to know that every time I hear the bell, someone has made a beneficial vow."

EXERCISE

Your Ceremony

When you have framed your personal vows, think of a way to have a ceremony to surround them. You could ask a spiritual teacher to help and friends or family to witness and support you. The ritual needn't be complicated. There is a sample ceremony in appendix 2.

JOINING A LARGER VOW

> At the time I was arrested I had no idea it would turn into this. It was just a day like any other day. The only thing that made it significant was that the masses of the people joined in.
>
> —ROSA PARKS[5]

Rosa Parks's arrest in 1955 for refusing to give up her seat in the "colored section" of a bus sparked a 381-day bus boycott by more than forty thousand black residents of Montgomery, Alabama, and galvanized the nascent civil rights movement. Forty years later Congress awarded her a gold medal, calling her the "First Lady of Civil Rights," noting that "her quiet dignity ignited the most significant social movement in the history of the United States."[6]

It's not necessary to invent our own unique vow or to find a life purpose that no one else shares. We can save ourselves a lot of time and cogitation by joining a larger vow. One person's vow can bear big dividends as others are inspired to join in and carry that vow forward. Over five thousand people the world over, moved by the example of one frail woman, Mother Teresa of Calcutta, have been ordained into her order and have committed their lives to serving the poor and ill. Over two hundred thousand people joined Martin Luther King in the nonviolent march on Washington in 1963, contributing to the eventual desegregation of schools and to the Civil Rights and Voting Rights Acts of the mid-1960s. These problems are not solved, and we are unlikely to live to see them completely solved, but each person who marched contributed to a great movement forward in recognizing and safeguarding the rights of those who need extra protection in order to enjoy a life of freedom and happiness.

In 1666 the Great Fire destroyed 80 percent of the homes in the city of London. St. Paul's Cathedral, built in the eleventh century over the course of 160 years, was destroyed. The great architect Christopher Wren was hired to rebuild the cathedral. Work started in 1669, when Wren was 37 years old, and the first service was held in the church when he was 65. He received the second half of his promised salary at age 79, when the church was completed. Who among us would have a vow powerful enough to continue working on a project for 32 years, on half salary!

There is an interesting story from the time of the rebuilding of St. Paul's. One morning, Wren, who was not personally known by many of the workers, stopped and asked three different laborers, all engaged in the same task, what they were doing.

The first said, "I am cutting this stone."

The second answered, "I am earning three shillings, six pence a day."

The third man straightened up, squared his shoulders, and still holding his mallet and chisel, replied, "I am helping Sir Christopher Wren build this great cathedral."

This story is often quoted in inspirational speeches. It inspires us because we want our brief life to have a purpose larger than selling people things they don't really need, larger than buying more things we don't really need, or larger than taking home a salary that is a bit bigger this year than last. Actually we want the life of *every* person to have a larger purpose. We don't want anyone to fall into the quicksand of despair and begin to feel that all human life is meaningless, ultimately finding no reason to live.

The Japanese people were in despair in the early eighth century, following ten years of freak weather, poor crops, famines, two attempts to overthrow the government, and a smallpox epidemic that killed all four sons of the Fujiwara regent. These chaotic conditions forced the emperor to move and rebuild the capital four times in ten years. In 743, in the hope of offering spiritual protection from further catastrophes, the emperor issued an edict ordering laypeople to help construct temples throughout the provinces. A monk named Gyogi rallied thousands of distressed and displaced people in this effort. For years Gyogi had been condemned by the religious establishment because he and his disciples did not conform with the harsh civil and religious laws of the times. His followers were a powerful force. He was an inspiring itinerant Buddhist priest, and whole towns turned out to hear him when he was preaching nearby. When unendurable levels of taxation forced thousands of farmers to abandon their lands, many had become priests under Gyogi. Gyogi and his army of supporters carried out scores of public works projects, building what the government had not: a main road, two ferry depots, three aqueducts, four canals, six bridges, nine charity houses, fifteen ponds, and forty-nine chapels.

The emperor commanded the construction of a giant Buddha statue. Gyogi and his students traveled around the country, gathering donations of money and jewelry to be melted into the figure. More than two and a half million people helped in the eight-year effort to cast the fifty-foot Great Buddha and build its huge hall—until recently the largest wooden building in the world. They were sustained more by their spiritual purpose than by their meager pay. Despite earthquakes and fires, the project was completed after eight years. Today, after twelve hundred years, the Great Buddha and Tōdai-ji Temple still inspire awe, and have become a UNESCO World Heritage Site. Because of the beneficial results of Gyogi's strong vows and his care for the common people, he became revered in Japan as an enlightened being, a bodhisattva.[7]

There are countless contemporary examples of one person's personal vow becoming a movement that inspires many others. Rachel O'Neill's strong intention was sparked by a trip to Malawi, Africa, where over one million children have been orphaned by HIV/AIDS, and many young girls are raising their siblings. She noticed that girls often had only one or two pieces of tattered clothing. She felt that the girls' clothing reflected their plight—poor, devalued, and uneducated, subjected to sexual abuse, and rendered permanently incontinent or dying in childbirth. Rachel decided to make simple dresses for the girls in several villages, "to plant in their hearts that they are worthy." Thousands of people from the United States, United Kingdom, Canada, Mexico, and Australia have joined Little Dresses for Africa, sewing over three million dresses made from pillowcases following simple online instructions.[8]

Vows are packets of energy. Energy is neither created nor destroyed. It can be transmuted into other forms. For example, the energy of heat can transform into mechanical energy in a steam engine that propels a ship. Similarly, the vow energies called nonviolence and love for one's enemy transformed into different forms as they animated the lives of South Africa's archbishop Desmond Tutu and Burmese peace activist Aung San Suu Kyi. This is the way vows are carried forward. They are picked up and passed from person to person, in circles of influence that continue to widen, unhindered, through space and time.

When we founded our monastery, a man in his sixties, not in good health, sold his house and moved to be near us. He had been in the Peace Corps twice and later worked as a house painter. Over the course of ten years, he has painted the inside and outside of the entire monastery and cast many religious statues. He said, "I wanted to do something useful with my remaining life energy, and I couldn't think of anything better to do than helping to found a monastery. I know it will benefit thousands of people in years to come."

The vow of a single person, multiplied through time and space, can affect the entire world. This applies to everyone, famous or obscure. The law of karma, of cause and effect, operates regardless of whether the world has recognized us as an "important person." Our vows are important because everything we do counts. Every action matters.

EXERCISES

Joining a Larger Vow

1. You have joined larger vows in the past. Think back to the organizations you have joined, contributed to, or served through volunteer work or service on their board. What were the vows these organizations embodied? Is there a theme common to these organizations that may reflect your underlying life vow? Here are examples from my life.

ORGANIZATIONS JOINED OR SERVED	VOWS EMBODIED BY ORGANIZATION OR WORK
Korean orphanage	Care and love for abandoned children
American Academy of Pediatrics	Good health care and loving environment for all children
Volunteer music teacher	Inspire children to play and enjoy music
Hospital child abuse program	Medical and psychological care for abused and neglected children
Donate to children's funds	Food and education for children living in poverty

2. List organizations you think will have a lasting and beneficial effect upon the world's suffering. Consider joining and
becoming part of their larger vow.

THE CHALLENGES VOWS PRESENT

VOWS ARE ALIVE, VOWS CHANGE

After Vatican II, we were directed to study and look more deeply into our vows.

—SUSAN, a Catholic nun

PEOPLE ARE SOMETIMES reluctant to make life vows because they worry about being locked into a vow permanently. Vows are not inflexible. They are *life* vows, and therefore they are alive. As our life changes, they grow and adapt too.

I interviewed Susan, a nun who entered her order right after high school graduation. She had grown up in a devout Catholic family of seven that knelt together by the couch each night to pray the rosary. She grew up with nuns as teachers and thought they seemed happy. In fourth grade she made an altar to Mary in her bedroom, offered flowers from her mother's garden, and knelt there to pray. In her sophomore year, she saw a film in catechism class about religious vocations. A scene of nuns at prayer catalyzed her decision to enter the religious life.

Soon after she made this decision, she was sitting on a heat register on the floor trying to stay warm, when she felt "a wordless, felt sense of God. It was an overwhelming sense of Presence. There was no voice—I went up to my bedroom and knelt down. I didn't pray. I just felt the desire to serve this Presence."

She entered the convent at age seventeen, fully expecting to wear a long black habit, veil, and blinders her entire life, and never to be able to go home to visit her family again. However, in her second year, the reforms of Vatican II were introduced by a progressive novice mistress, and the strict and secluded life of the nuns became more open.

At one point, before taking final vows, Susan was struggling with the question of whether she had enough faith to become a nun. Suddenly she felt the sense of Presence again, and she realized that faith in herself was not the issue. She had what she needed—trust in that great Presence.

She took final vows at age twenty. Her three primary religious vows were poverty, chastity, and obedience. Poverty included sharing, simplicity, and stewardship. Sharing meant that everything belonged to the order and was a common resource. No one owned anything. Everything was referred to as "ours," including each woman's toothbrush. Poverty also implied simplicity. The novices slept in rows in a dormitory, separated by curtains. Each space had a bed, a dresser, and a chair. Each woman had a long black dress, a watch, a Bible, and several changes of underclothing. If she needed something, anything, she had to ask. Stewardship meant a responsibility to care for all gifts, which meant *everything*. Obedience meant the nuns were obedient to their superiors in the convent and to the regional superior. The nuns "went where we were sent." Susan was posted to various Catholic elementary schools, where she taught for eighteen years.

The vow of chastity was originally rule-based. Sisters wore the holy habit as a practice of modesty. They were not allowed to go out without another sister or chaperone. They were discouraged from having personal friends, even among the other nuns. Spirit and body were seen as separate, and the body was seen as the source of (troublesome) fleshly desires. Education about the role of sexuality was not part of formation. An intimate relationship with Jesus and God was primary, and the nuns wore a wedding ring to show that they were unavailable for marriage.

After the reforms of the Second Vatican Council of 1962–65, nuns were directed to study and deepen their understanding of the charism of their order and of their vows. As they looked more deeply into the underlying intention and benefit of the vows, the vows changed.

The nuns began to wear street clothing. Susan relates that the vow of poverty is still based upon living simply and sharing communal property, such as kitchens, cars, and lawnmowers, but with the aspiration to be good stewards of the earth and its gifts. In her order, each nun draws up a personal budget for the year and manages her own finances.

The vow of obedience has evolved from passive assent into the active practice of individual and communal discernment. She says it implies listening to one's conscience and considering how your decision will affect others in the group. The order's constitution and the Gospels serve as guides. Each nun has the ability to plan what work she wants to get involved in but must solicit input from the members of the community and even the provincial. They believe that the Holy Spirit is actively guiding them, through contemplative prayer, through their own receptive hearts, and through their leaders. There is also communal discernment of gifts, as in discovering who among the nuns has the gift for leadership, for that particular time and issue.

The vow of chastity also evolved. It was still focused on love for God, but more actively expressed in the nuns' lives, through prayer, through discovering God's presence in (loving) other people and in nature. Susan describes the new view of celibacy as a gift, life giving and creative, that allows the sexual energy that is usually channeled into one exclusive relationship to flow outward in a nonsexual form and enrich many relationships, with people and with nature. Ultimately it becomes service that, following the example of Jesus, is directed to people on the margins, not valued by society.

Susan's vows are multifaceted. They are part of the larger vows of her religious community within the Catholic church. They are vows for more than this lifetime, both as her individual life continues after death and as the order's vows continue. They are inspired vows, inspired by her family's faith, by the nuns she knew personally, by the movie she saw in school, and by several experiences of what she calls the Presence.

After forty-seven years as a nun, at the end of a Zen retreat focused on discerning one's vows, Susan summarized her vows with a simple phrase from her childhood catechism: "To know, to love, and to serve God in this world and the next." She says, "The innate desire to know God was part of my being since very early on. I know less about what God is now, but I want to act out of faith and trust in that Presence so that it becomes a source of wisdom and compassion in me."

Vows are not static. They are alive and will grow and change as our experience of life expands and as our understanding of our life's purpose deepens. It helps to study our vows periodically, as the nuns did, to free them from the confines of rote recitation and to allow them to become once again both an active force and an underlying, stable presence in our lives. Some vows may be set aside, some vows will be transformed, and sometimes new vows will be born.

EXERCISES

1. Morning Vow Awareness

For one week, say your vows silently each morning. Be aware of whether some vows need revising. Be aware of whether it might be possible to look more deeply into a vow.

2. Periodic Vow Review

Pick a time of year to reflect on and possibly revise your vows. You could pick a time when you are more aware of the changing, flowing nature of life, such as your birthday or the New Year. It helps to attend a silent retreat, so you have freedom from daily demands and can develop greater clarity and objectivity in your mind. At our monastery we do a life vows retreat for this purpose each January.

VOWS AFTER RETIREMENT

When my father-in-law retired from the furniture business, he found new purpose in chasing down bargains. He would drive across town to save ten cents on a gallon of milk. Since he was living on limited funds, this was his way of continuing to support the spouse he loved. Other retired friends have spent their time cruising and sightseeing, on ships or in campers. Others have settled down to a contented life of taping television shows and e-mailing cartoons and funny videos to friends and relatives.

Retirement can be difficult if you are not clear about your life vows. I asked a friend about how her husband's recent retirement was going. She rolled her eyes and said, "Well, he's just hanging around the house and doesn't know what to do with himself." This seems to be an issue for many men, faced each morning with a life that seems devoid of purpose after they have retired or lost their job. This is another example of the importance of life vows—and the difficulty people have if they mistake their job for their life purpose. A job is not the purpose. It is the means to carry out that purpose.

I interviewed my friend's husband, Dan, about his life purpose. He said that his vow had always been to support his family. He had grown up with seven siblings, and his father had worked very hard to earn enough money just to provide his large family with the basics of food, shelter, and clothing. The children began working to earn money for school clothes by age ten, picking strawberries and blueberries during the summer.

Dan had worked his way up through a large paper company, becoming an accountant as a way to ensure that money was carefully husbanded and spent—a motive that hints of a reactive vow. He retired after thirty-five years and found himself at loose ends, running errands and doing small jobs around the house. We talked about how he had provided well for his children, now grown, and now he could expand the field of his caretaking and use his skills to provide these same benefits—the security of adequate food, shelter, and clothing—to other families.

We brainstormed. He could do volunteer work with food banks or with homeless shelters. He could become an unpaid treasurer for a church or other nonprofit. He could help a family emerge from poverty by lending money through a microfinancing organization, such as KIVA. He could work through SCORE, a fifty-year-old organization of volunteers who give seasoned advice on all aspects of starting or expanding small businesses. What he could offer others doesn't even have to be related to his old job. He could develop a new skill. For example, if he liked to sing, he could join a Threshold Choir and offer soothing music at the bedsides of people who are dying.

For many people there is something unsatisfying about retiring the skills you have honed and the knowledge you have gained over many years and often at significant cost, and just puttering about or checking off new countries on your to-see list. In that case, it can help to discern the underlying vows that directed your life and see if you could be creative, find a new venue, and continue to carry them out. Because people are living longer, there is time for an "encore career" and a number of organizations, and even fellowships, to help you find or train for it.

EXERCISE

How to Carry on a Life Vow after Retirement

Here is a list of jobs. Think of how the skills developed in each job could be used in retirement to continue to benefit others. I'll give you one example.

JOB	HOW THOSE SKILLS COULD BENEFIT OTHERS IN RETIREMENT
Restaurant cook	Volunteer to cook once a week at a domestic-violence shelter
	Teach kids who have eaten only processed food how to cook using fresh ingredients
	Bake and wrap cookies and hand them out to homeless people
Bus driver	
Schoolteacher	
Musician	
Computer technician	
Mother	
Editor	
Artist	
Landscaper	
Therapist	
Doctor or nurse	
Custodian	

WHEN OUR VOWS ARE CHALLENGED

What is to give light must endure burning.

—VIKTOR FRANKL, Holocaust survivor and psychiatrist[1]

You know how when things seem to be going along exceptionally well for quite a long time, and just as you begin to think that you've finally learned to flow in accord with your path in life, then . . . a big problem arises. And it's a surprise, not anything you had anticipated, and it seems bigger than you think you can chew, swallow, and digest.

This is the real test of our vows. If we take our vows seriously, our vows will take *us* seriously. They will bring us exactly what we need to work with, in order for the vow to work cleanly within us and in the world.

A vow is not a pretty phrase we write and send off in a greeting card or stick to the refrigerator door with a magnet until it falls off and slides underneath, unnoticed. If we are earnest in our vows, they become an active practice.

A carpenter friend took on the life vow of "being openhearted in all situations." A few weeks later, he went to the bank to deposit a check that a customer had given him for cabinetry work. He waited in line and presented the check and deposit slip to the young cashier, with a request for some cash back. As she stamped the deposit slip, she told him that the check wouldn't clear for a few days. My friend told her he needed the money that day to pay his rent. She repeated the facts about when the funds would be available. He lost his temper, yelled at her, using profanity about the banking business, and stalked out. When he got home, he reflected on what had happened. He felt badly about losing his temper and saw its downstream effects. He realized he had frightened the clerk and several other customers.

He recalled his vow. Here he had a choice. In recalling his vow, he could have become angry at himself and felt even more miserable. This is what the Buddha called "the second dart." We are shot with one dart, and instead of pulling it out, we shoot ourselves with another dart. The first dart was his fear about what would happen if he couldn't pay his rent on time. The second dart was the anger he unleashed on the young bank teller. If he had become angry at himself for being angry, that would have been the third dart, doubling the anger—not a good strategy. Instead of feeling upset with himself, he recalled his vow and decided he must follow it. He meditated until the fear and anger dissolved and his heart was open again. Then he went back to the bank and spoke warmly, apologizing to the startled clerk.

If we've taken on a big vow, we may not be able to manifest it in a certain difficult moment. But we can recall it and be guided by it as we ponder what repair work to do. This is keeping the vow, in a powerful way. Our vow will test us, and if we face and pass the test, our faith in the vow and in ourselves as the carrier of the vow will grow.

Here is an example of a vow challenge. A person I mentored for many years left our organization and began talking negatively to others, telling them to keep it confidential. This created a very unpleasant atmosphere, corroded by secrecy, and divided a formerly cohesive group.

My first vow is to become enlightened. How does that vow apply here? Enlightenment is composed of a balance of two energies, openhearted compassion and clear-minded wisdom. As the vow is tested, it springs to life. It becomes a very dynamic activity, hour by hour. I stay alert to the activity in my heart-mind. Any time I detect that my mind is turning toward the problem and begins to be tainted with resentment, I work to clear the heaviness in my heart and to stop the negative thoughts from spiraling and expanding. I pick up my tools and use them with urgent purpose, doing loving-kindness practice for myself and for the other person, working to dissolve any traces of negative inner talk, and cultivating kindness in my heart toward the accuser.

At the same time, I must work with clarity of mind to investigate the source of this person's unhappiness, to corral their destructive behavior, to investigate my own behavior with objectivity, to see what changes I need to make, and to respond to the secondary distress in the community. Clarity and compassion—working together like the right foot and left foot in walking. This is easy to write, but not easy to do.

In 733 four ships left Japan for a perilous four-month journey to China. The several ambassadors and priests onboard were sent by the Japanese government to invite a master to return to Japan to give the Buddhist precepts and establish an organization to train well-qualified priests. When, after nine years of travel around China, they had not found such a master, the priests petitioned Ganjin, who, at fifty-four, was already famous throughout China. Ganjin asked his assembled monks, "There is a country where Buddhism is destined to flourish. Who among my followers will respond to that invitation and set out for Japan, there to transmit the dharma?" The monks were silent. Finally, one priest spoke: "That country is exceedingly far away, and it is difficult to arrive there safely. In a hundred sailings, less than one is successful. The human body is hard to acquire and to be born in China is even more difficult . . . therefore all followers remain silent and do not answer." Ganjin replied, "This is for the good of the dharma. A Buddhist should not care about risking his life. Since none of you will go, I will go myself."[2]

In 743 he set out for Japan, but the ship was seized. The next two attempts failed when their ships were driven ashore by storms. The fourth try was subverted by Ganjin's followers. In 748 he set out again, but the ship was blown off course and shipwrecked. The passengers nearly died of dehydration and starvation, and as a result Ganjin eventually went blind. In 753, eleven years after his first attempt, after thirty-six of his original traveling companions had died, Ganjin finally arrived in Japan. He was welcomed by both the government and the people, bestowed with rice fields to sustain the

monastics at his temples, and given full responsibility for the ordi-
nation of all Buddhist nuns and monks. He trained priests and
nuns diligently until his death at age seventy-five.

Whenever I encounter obstacles to fulfilling my vows, I remember Ganjin.

Another challenge to practicing with vows can occur when our
life circumstances change. Such a challenge usually means that we
need to broaden the definition of our vows or the means we are
using to accomplish them. A woman had been practicing diligently,
frequently attending weeklong silent retreats. She became pregnant, a happy event, but after the baby was born, she became sad,
realizing she could not devote much time even to daily meditation,
let alone long retreats. Would enlightenment ever be possible? Her
teacher instructed her to go on a weeklong retreat in a small hermit-
age hut, with the baby. These were the meditation instructions he
gave her: Pay close attention to the baby. Learn all you can about this
new human being. By changing the kind of meditation practice she
was doing, she and the baby had a very happy and intimate retreat
together.

If our vow is to awaken and our means to that awakening has
been silent seated meditation, if circumstances make us unable to
do long introspective sitting, we can become discouraged, thinking
we have fallen away from our vow. In that case we have to remember
that one particular form of meditation is just the (current) means,
not the vow. Only the means has changed, and now we need to be
creative in finding other ways to carry out the vow.

At the hospital where I work, I encountered a nurse I hadn't seen
for a few years. She told me her husband had sustained a frontal-lobe
brain injury in a car accident, resulting in unfortunate changes in
his personality. His baseline had changed from happy to unhappy,
and he had sudden bursts of anger. The family was on edge trying to
detect and avoid what set him off. He needed a lot of extra care and
monitoring, and she was worried about the effect of his anger on
their two children. She wanted to keep her wedding vows but was

contemplating a separation. Ultimately she stayed with him, and after several years of rehabilitation, he has begun to recover and is working again. If he had not recovered, or if his angry outbursts had worsened, she might have moved out when her vows to raise her children in a loving and safe environment took precedence. I know, though, that she would have figured out a way to continue to honor her wedding vows, perhaps by hiring a kind caretaker for her impaired husband.

When I was an intern, working seventy-hour weeks, I had no time to meditate. In any posture, even standing up, if I closed my eyes for a few seconds, I fell asleep. I had to find ways to practice, to flow with awareness through the course of a busy day, while driving, eating, starting an IV in a preemie's tiny veins, listening to the lungs of a sick child, waiting for an elevator, climbing the stairs two at time when the elevator was too slow, entering the room where a code blue (signal for a patient trying to die on us) had been called. I had shifted the means from periodic meditation to ongoing mindfulness, but my vow was the same, to become enlightened. And it supported another vow, to relieve people's suffering by being a doctor.

Now I'm too old to work twenty-hour days, and I have seen that the key to relieving suffering lies in people's minds. I've met patients with terminal cancer whose hearts and minds were serene and content and people with colds or a headache who were anxious and miserable. Thus I've switched my means from working with the body (medicine) to working with the mind and heart (Zen teaching), but my vow remains the same, to relieve people's distress and unhappiness and ultimately to teach them how to do this for themselves.

Please be assured that when our ability to keep working with a vow seems challenged, the vow is working! It is working *on us,* to help us open up our view of that vow and to become more creative. It is testing our resolve, our resourcefulness, the depth of our understanding of this vow, and often, our sense of humor.

EXERCISE

When Your Vow Was Tested

This is a great exercise to do with a friend or in a group. Think of an example of how one of your vows has been tested. This is not so hard. Think of times when desire was strong and you were tempted to do something not in accord with your personal principles. If you are a parent, think about sleepless nights with new infants, sick children, and errant teens. If you are an older adult, think about when you cared for your elderly parents or relatives. Think about a time when a friend seemed to betray you or a promised or hoped-for outcome fell through.

What did you fall back on when your vows were tested? How do you think the test benefited you? What did you learn about yourself as a result of this test? How did the test affect or change your vow?

UNFINISHED VOWS

We cannot, after all, judge a biography by its length, by the number of pages in it; we must judge by the richness of the contents . . . Sometimes the "unfinished" are among the most beautiful symphonies.

—VIKTOR FRANKL[3]

When we think of our single lifetime as beginning at conception or birth and ending at death, we limit our view of vows. Vows become infused with anxiety. What if we die with no warning, before we accomplish our vows?

It is important to realize that we are not in control of all of cause and effect. And as we age we have to relinquish control of our bodies. When we were young, we could expect our bodies to follow our commands, more or less, but as we age, our bodies become recalci-trant, sagging downward in response to the inexorable pull of grav-ity, losing the ability to balance on one foot, run a mile, sleep all night without a trip to the bathroom, hear a whisper, or read small print in dim light. As we age, our minds, too, become less coopera-tive. They refuse to get up off the couch and get to work; they refuse to retrieve the memory files we need or even to think clearly. We can't remember nouns or proper names or dates of important events and, eventually, perhaps even the names of our own children.

How then can we work with our earnest intent to carry on our unfinished vows? There is a danger here that in our disappointment over not accomplishing all we had hoped in our lifetime, we will try to foist our unfinished vows off on our children. The mother of composer Nicolas Hodges was a professional opera singer who abandoned her career to have children. Nicolas was a musical prod-igy, but as a teen, when he told his parents he wanted to be a com-poser, not a pianist, he said, "It was like I'd stabbed them. What I thought was all for and because of me was actually all for and be-cause of her. It became shockingly clear that my mother didn't care what I wanted at all."[4]

The piano prodigy Lang Lang told an interviewer, "Both of my parents had their music dreams. Somehow they achieved a little bit but not much. But they basically had the hope that their son would finish their childhood musical dreams."[5] His father practiced to become a professional player of the *erhu*, a Chinese traditional in-strument, but was forced to work in a factory during the Cultural Revolution in China. Lang Lang could sing before he could speak. His parents decided to train him and see what happened. His fa-ther imposed military discipline upon the child, and when at age nine he came home from a failed audition, his father beat him and gave him pills, telling Lang Lang to commit suicide. When Lang Lang refused, his father told him to jump off the building. Lang Lang began hitting his father, crying, "Why should I kill myself? I've done nothing wrong." The child vowed never to touch the piano again. Fortunately he befriended a vegetable peddler who made peace between Lang Lang and his father. The boy began playing again and became one of the best-known pianists in the world. He sometimes invites his father to play the erhu with him at concerts.[6]

Children who inherit their parents' vows are not always happy carrying out a vow that is not of their own creation, one that did not emerge naturally from their unique lives. I know several adults who inherited large sums of money, a gift from parents who had been successful in carrying out their own vows to acquire wealth and thus happiness and security. The parents believed the gift of wealth would enable their children to live a life unencumbered by the hard work their ancestors had undergone. However, these adult children were unhappy. With no meaningful work, they had no clear direction in life, not even the work one is forced to do to pay for food and shelter. They had difficulty with intimate relationships and were suspicious of anyone who wanted to come close, always wondering if the person truly liked them or was secretly after their money.

Some acquaintances once took in a woman friend who was dying. As her life energy waned, she became increasingly anxious about the things that would be left undone in her life. As each friend came to visit her, she would give them one of her unfinished projects to carry out, such as planting bulbs in her garden or finding a lost person in order to send a letter of apology. It was hard to refuse a friend on her deathbed, so they took these tasks on; but it was a burden, and people stopped coming to visit. We cannot expect others to carry out our vows after we die, which means that we have to be at peace with the fact that we will have unfinished vows.

We must realize that all large vows will be unfinished in our lifetime. We do the best we can to manifest them while we are able. It is reassuring to know that the energy of vows does not die when our body dies but will be picked up and carried forward by someone else or, perhaps, if rebirth does occur, picked up once again by us!

EXERCISE

Time Is Running Out

Imagine as vividly as you can that you have been given three years to live. Are there unfinished projects that you would like to complete in those three years? List them. Are there unfinished projects that you would discard immediately? List them. How do those projects relate to your primary life vows? With time drawing short, is there anything new that you would undertake? Consider each of these realms: travel, making amends, visiting old friends or out-of-touch family, doing something daring, learning a new skill, spiritual work, or retreats.

VOWS THAT CONTINUE FOR LIFETIMES

My life often seemed to me like a story that has no beginning and no end . . . I could well imagine that I might have lived in former centuries and there encountered questions I was not yet able to answer; that I had been born again because I had not fulfilled the task given to me. When I die my deeds will follow along with me . . . It is important to ensure that I do not stand at the end with empty hands.

—CARL JUNG[7]

From the moment I first heard it, I recognized Renaissance music as "my music." Just to hear a few notes makes me happy. I learned to play recorder, so I could immerse myself in it. My parents were from the American South and played gospel music on the record player. Where did my instant affinity for music composed over five hundred years ago on another continent come from? Even stranger, how did I, a Protestant girl from upstate New York, end up wearing Tang dynasty Chinese robes over a Japanese kimono over American underwear, living in a Zen monastery in Oregon?

Here's a possible answer to the last question. I was born on the day that Nagasaki was bombed, three days after Hiroshima met the same fate. Thousands of people died in those Japanese cities in the few days around my birth. My first breath must have contained the dust of their vaporized bodies. Many who died were Buddhist priests and nuns. Did I also take in their hopes, their unfinished vows? Could it be that we are "infected" before birth with fragments of another person's passions, their loves and hates?

Although this might be a disturbing idea, that we are made up of parts of other people and beings or that we are *only* made up of what we call "others," it makes sense from a biological point of view. The calcium in my bones is very, very old. It was created not long after the Big Bang, and in the intervening 13.8 billion years, it became part of countless bodies, animals, plants, and people, before being incorporated into my teeth and bones. After I die, "my" calcium will be passed on to innumerable other beings, becoming blades of grass, then the tiny bones of the mouse that hides within them, and then the feathers of the hungry owl that swoops down upon the mouse. Some of my calcium may trickle down through the watershed and out into the ocean, to be incorporated into the shells of small sea creatures. Countless beings eventually will inherit "my" calcium, even in bits as small as one molecule, and some, like the beetles that chew my bone dust, may inherit bigger clumps of my calcium.

The law that energy is neither created nor destroyed should apply to all forms of energy, not only physical energy. Could it be that smaller or larger "clumps" of mental-emotional energy can also be passed and thus influence people in the future? Could the vows of a priest who died in Nagasaki have entered my nascent consciousness the day I was born?

When my husband and I founded the monastery where we live, our teacher, Harada Roshi, advised us to build it to last for a thousand years. This is a vow that cannot be fulfilled in one lifetime. It must be passed on, generation after generation.

The great cathedrals of Europe were built by people who knew that they were not likely to live long enough to see the completion of the building. Some workers and several generations of their descendants spent their entire lives completing just one part of the church. The beautiful Orvieto Cathedral in Italy was begun in 1290 and took nearly three centuries to complete. A succession of ten architects and hundreds of stonemasons, carpenters, sculptors, and painters worked on the building. As architectural styles evolved, the design of the cathedral underwent many revisions. One sculptor spent eight years just carving a large marble Pietà for the church!

Jon Kabat-Zinn tells of seeing a poster for a talk on Zen meditation when he was a young graduate student. The talk was given by Roshi Philip Kapleau, one of the first Westerners to teach Zen in America. Although there were only three people in the audience, Kapleau spoke with vigor and Jon was riveted. He went on to develop Mindfulness-Based Stress Reduction (MBSR), a secular form of meditation that relieves pain and stress and supports physical and emotional healing. MBSR has spread around the world, into hospitals, schools, corporations, and prisons. Roshi Kapleau died without knowing the effect of this one wholehearted, vow-inspired talk.

We must formulate and carry out our vows in the faith that there will be benefit, for one person or ten or for millions, in centuries to come.

For the time being, the calcium energy, the Nagasaki vow energy, the love of the music of Praetorius—all are part of a bundle I call "me." In the future, for another time being, it will become the building blocks of many other beings. If we see that our energy, physical and psychical, will not die but will be passed on, inherited by countless beings for millions of years to come, what would we like to do with it while we are in its possession? I think we would like to clean it up, so it can be passed on in even a slightly better form. How can we do that? I could clean up what will be passed on of my body's physical energy by eating in a healthy way, avoiding pesticides and radioactivity, for example. How to clean up my mental-emotional energy, so that, when I pass out of time, I can bequeath to other beings still living in time more kindness, more wisdom, more humility than I find in myself? That kind of cleaning, that kind of transformation, is the domain of spiritual practice.

A Passion for Dance

At age fifteen Anusha bought an unusual statue that she saw in a shop window. She couldn't explain why it intrigued her. A few years later, a woman came to Anusha's college class in costume to do a demonstration of classical Indian dance. Immediately Anusha thought, "I can do that." She told me, "It was very strange, as I wasn't a physical person at all. I hated physical education, and, being a second-generation Canadian, I wanted to be Western. But I was immediately intrigued with this dance." She found a very good teacher and began intensive practice, three lessons a week, and solo practice every morning. She credits dance with saving her life at a time when she was suffering acute grief from the death of her two best friends and her parents' divorce. "I discovered the joy of being, of moving, in a body. I feel most peaceful, most powerful, and most intimate with myself and everything when I'm working on a dance piece."

She learned that the statue was of the Indian god Shiva, dancing in flames. She felt she'd been given a great gift, to become a conduit for this ancient tradition. Her teacher's generosity inspired her to teach, but instead of following his example and taking only the most talented students, she takes anyone, including people who have physical dyslexia. She loves her work and says she has seen people's lives transformed by just one hour a week of dancing.

Anusha's family is from Sri Lanka, a country where belief in rebirth is usual. Thus it is easy for her to consider that her love for a foreign dance form was inherited from someone in another country, in another time.

A Passion for Japanese Prints

"I can't explain why I have such a passion for this one artist's prints." I was interviewing Marc, a sixty-five-year-old American computer consultant, about the underlying purpose(s) of his life. We had talked about his primary goal in raising his two daughters, to endow them with healthy self-esteem. Marc's daughters were now grown, and I was curious about an unusual aspect of his life. I had met him while square dancing and been surprised to discover that he is a determined collector of two unique things, small round wooden boxes made on Miyajima, an island off Hiroshima, and the woodblock prints of Takahashi Shōtei, a little-known Japanese artist who died in 1945.

How had his passion begun? There were two threads. When he was in college, a friend invited him to an exhibit of prints by a then-unknown Dutch artist. Marc was too poor to purchase any prints, but his friend bought two for about fifty dollars each. He later sold these prints, which were by Escher, and bought a house with the proceeds. Marc made an inner promise—a reactive vow—not to pass up such an opportunity again. The second thread he traces to his wife, who treasured two round wooden boxes she'd inherited from her mother. Marc bought a few more boxes online as gifts for his wife and traced the image of the tall gate carved on one box to the famous *torii** gates that stand in the water on Miyajima, an island that is sacred to the Shinto religion. He began to search for a woodblock print of the gate online, and this led him to a print that "instantly spoke" to him.

A passion was ignited, and now, fifteen years later, he has over two hundred prints by the little-known Japanese artist Shōtei. He has a website devoted to this artist and is able instantly to recognize prints by Shōtei that have been attributed to another printmaker. He has developed friends in the Japanese print world and is learning Japanese. He cannot give a rational explanation for his devotion to this artist. When I mentioned rebirth as a possible mechanism, this reserved, middle-aged computer consultant immediately said, "It's the only thing that makes sense."

For some people it is reassuring to frame their unexplained passions as a strong energy that was inherited from someone else in the past. For some people this is disturbing. They want to form their own hobbies or infatuations. This is interesting to consider. What if all of our strong vows were inherited from "someone else"?

EXERCISES

1. Determining Prebirth Influences

If possible, do this exercise with a partner or group. Consider each question, and then discuss your answers.

Do you have any strong interests that are not explained by—or even run counter to—the interests of your family or upbringing? Where do you think it came from? If this passion were passed on to you by someone who lived before you were born, would that be disturbing or intriguing to you?

2. Vow Energy after This Life

Consider that when you die, your vow energy will not die but will be taken up by someone who does not live in this place or time. How do you feel about that possibility?

WHEN VOWS ARE BROKEN

Remember,
in this place
no one can hear you

and out of this silence
you can make a promise
it will kill you to break,

that way you'll find
what is real and what is not.

—DAVID WHYTE, "All the True Vows"[8]

My first teacher, Maezumi Roshi, made a distinction between "breaking" your vows and "getting them muddy." By "breaking" your vows he meant that when you made the vow, you did not actually have the intention to keep the vow. When you broke the vow, it was permanently broken, since it had almost no presence in your life to begin with. For example, sociopaths may make promises without any intention of keeping them long-term.

On the other hand, Maezumi Roshi said that getting our vows muddy was inevitable. If you walk around outside, eventually your new shoes will get dirty and lose their shine. You just notice that they are dirty and clean them. If you walk around living life, it will be impossible to keep your vows perfectly. They will become tarnished. No one can keep a large vow perfectly all the time, in every circumstance. You just notice that they have become unclear and renew them, so they have a fresh presence in your life again.

In Zen we take sixteen precepts, guidelines for living a beneficial life. The sixth is "not to gossip." For many people, this is not an easy vow to keep. In fact, at the Zen Center in Los Angeles we had a box marked #6, and anytime you caught yourself gossiping, you had to put a quarter in. We collected enough for a party. The point is not to give up, but to recollect the vow, notice that we've muddied it, and clean it up by remaking our commitment to the vow again.

Some people start out motivated by one vow and abruptly discover that it has not worked out as they thought. Their vow has had unexpected and troubling consequences.

A friend told me of two young men who volunteered to join the military after the 9/11 terrorist attacks. After a few months of basic training, one of the young men called his father in crisis, saying, "Please get us a good lawyer. We are going AWOL. They have us marching around, shouting, 'Kill, kill, kill!' They are training us to kill anyone, including women and children, for fear they might be carrying incendiary devices. We've gone to our commanding officer to say why we are not willing to do this, but no one will listen. We have to leave." These young men enlisted with strong vows to protect their homeland, their town, their family and friends. Then they discovered that what they were being trained to do was contrary to their more primary vow, not to kill innocent people. Ultimately they decided to face the consequences of breaking the promises they'd made upon enlistment and their oaths of obedience to their commanders.

We think we are lucky in this country because war and its horrors have not invaded our national boundaries, but actually they have. They have invaded insidiously, in the minds, bodies, and hearts of those who have fought in wars and returned. These men have been instructed to violate the first commandment or precept of all major religions, not to kill another human being. Once you have been trained to break the primary ethical precept, it becomes more difficult not to let all the basic precepts go. These men have left home and gone abroad to kill, not just terrorists or enemy soldiers, as they thought, but also innocent civilians. Because no one can be sure who the enemy is and because shots and bombs and missiles go astray, because they have been ordered to drive straight on for fear of hidden explosive devices, they have killed infants in their mothers' arms, cowering women, toothless, helpless old people, and laughing children who ran toward their military vehicles.

They return home with their minds invaded by guilt, shame, and violent anger, and a sense of betrayal. They followed their vows, doing what they were ordered to do, and in doing so, they have lost their moral compass. Even if they escaped physical injury, they may bear deep spiritual wounds. This may be why more men (and women) in the armed services die of suicide than in combat. They have to be helped to find a new vow, one that will help them, as they carry it out, to restore their spiritual health, to recover their hope and faith, and to integrate their hearts back into their being.

When we face the possibility of breaking a vow, it is important to investigate whether that vow is actually a vow or a means. The two young men who enlisted wished to protect their country and their families from violence until they realized that they themselves were being trained to become violent and could eventually present more of a threat to their families than a terrorist half a world away. Enlisting was a means, not a primary vow.

Sometimes a vow is causing harm. When that is seen, then breaking the vow is crucial. A dramatic example occurred in the years soon after A.D. 33, when a man named Paul was traveling from Jerusalem to Syria in order to arrest, interrogate, and possibly execute the followers of a new religious cult based upon the teaching of a man named Jesus. A bright light suddenly knocked him to the ground and blinded him for three days. He heard a voice that commanded him to proceed to Damascus, where his sight was restored and he underwent conversion, becoming an ardent missionary for Christianity. His original vow, to eradicate Christianity, was discarded, and he took up a new vow, preaching and spreading that religion in Greece, Rome, Spain, and Asia Minor.

Parents often face the dilemma of loving a child and doing something painful or distressing to the child. They may have to give a diabetic child shots, forbid fun but dangerous pastimes, enforce time-outs, or report the child's wrongdoing to the principal or police. These actions are undertaken not out of anger or dislike, but as the means to carry out the parent's primary vow, to love and support the child's optimal health and growth.

People with good intentions may find themselves in a situation where they discover that their life mission, intended to do good, is actually causing harm. Because of his linguistic talent, Daniel Everett[9] was dispatched as a Christian missionary to the Amazon to work with the Pirahã tribe. Two previous missionaries had spent two decades there, failing to master the Pirahã language, which is unrelated to any other language, or to interest the Pirahã in Christianity. Everett learned Pirahã and translated and read books of the Bible to them, without effect. Now, after thirty years of living with the tribe of about 350 people, he relates that they "exist almost completely in the present. Absorbed by the daily struggle to survive, they do not plan ahead, store food, build houses or canoes to last, maintain tools or talk of things beyond those that they, or people they know, have experienced." Everett became intrigued by the Pirahã people's view of truth and came to see his religion as "coercive" and lost his faith. As a result he also lost his wife (who still evangelizes among the tribe and was the first to observe that the Pirahã language has sung and hummed forms) and contact with his three children. His findings have stirred up an as-yet unresolved controversy among linguists about whether the basics of language are biologically or culturally based.

Everett has concluded that "It's wrong to try and convert tribal societies. What should the empirical evidence for religion be? It should produce peaceful, strong, secure people who are right with God and right with the world. I don't see that evidence very often. So then I find myself with the Pirahã. They have all these qualities that I am trying to tell them they could have. They are the ones who are living life the way I'm saying it ought to be lived, they just don't fear heaven and hell."

Everett's experiences transformed his life purpose. He gave up endeavoring to convert the Pirahã to a Western religion and became more interested in understanding these unusual people and the implications of their worldview for how better to live a human life.

ATONEMENT

If you have muddied your vows, it is important to admit and confess, to yourself and at least one other person, what you have done. In Zen we call this *atonement*. It means that we let go of the denial that separates us from what we have done. We hold it as part of us, and then we let it go, with a renewed vow to realign our lives with what is wholesome and beneficial.

Atonement—or "at one-ment"—implies that you, your actions, and the effect of your actions are all one. Atonement work involves acknowledging (to a religious or spiritual leader, sponsor, or therapist) that you have not kept your vows, taking full responsibility for any resultant harm and looking for a way to repair that harm. If you cannot make amends directly with the person you harmed, you can write a letter (and send it or not) and do some kind of reparation work with your body. At the monastery we dedicate portions of our practice, extra chants or extra bows, to those we know we have harmed and to anyone we may have harmed, even inadvertently.

It is important to have a conscience, a voice inside that tells us when we have done something unskillful and against our vows. It is *very* important not to let what we have done become a heavy burden of shame or guilt that prevents us from making amends, learning from our mistakes, and moving forward.

Breaking a vow does not mean that we are broken. Breaking—or muddying—a vow can enable us to understand more deeply the importance of that vow and renew our determination to keep it more carefully in the future.

EXERCISE

Atonement

Think of a time you did or said something, even inadvertently, that caused harm. Think of the underlying vow or central value that you violated when you did this.

Do atonement. Here is simple way.

"I acknowledge that I have muddied/broken my vows."

"I acknowledge that I have caused harm through my speech and actions. "

"I dedicate any merit from these bows/these chants/my meditation today to _____ (the person I harmed). May (he or she) be at ease in body and mind."

6

THE VOWS OF RELATIONSHIPS

MARRIAGE AND DIVORCE

To have and to hold from this day forward, for better, for worse, for richer, for poorer, in sickness and in health, to love and cherish, until we are parted by death. This is my solemn vow.

—EPISCOPAL WEDDING VOWS

WHEN MOST PEOPLE hear the word *vow*, they think of marriage vows. These are probably the most formal and public vows that people take during their lives. However, the divorce rate in the United States is about 50 percent, and when I offer classes on forming life vows, I find that some divorced people, disappointed in themselves or the institution of marriage, are cautious about undertaking any further vows. They can hear an inner critical voice saying, "You failed to keep your vows when you got married. You cannot keep vows. Don't bother to take on another vow and risk another failure."

Some people take marriage vows with every intention of staying married for the rest of their lives. Others take marriage vows with a small "reserved" area in the back of their minds. This reserved area contains a back door, an emergency exit in case the relationship encounters difficulties that one or both partners don't want to look in the face and work out. Marriage vows give us the extra incentive to make a serious attempt to work it out. Vows also give us a chance to give ourselves—and our notions of how things should be—a workout.

Many people take sincere vows to love someone forever. When the romantic love runs out, or when they break up, they feel guilty that they have broken their vow of eternal love. We have to look at this more deeply.

What does it mean to love someone? Is it a certain excited feeling in the body or the area of the heart? Does it mean you feel happy with them and unhappy without them? Does it mean you want them to love only you and always to meet your needs? Is love a state of seeing and believing the best about someone? Or falling in love with the person our beloved believes us to be? To me love is an action. Love is the ongoing activity of supporting another person in developing to his or her highest potential, even if it means sacrificing something we ourselves want.

Could you continue to love someone in that way or grow to love someone in that way even after the romantic thrill fades? Could you wish and work for his or her good even after a mastectomy removes her lovely breast or prostate surgery leaves him impotent, even after Alzheimer's disease erases his or her memory of your happiness together, or after a divorce separates you? Vows are alive. Alive means growing and changing with circumstances, just like people do.

A friend overheard a young person comment at a wedding, "Oh, he'll be OK as a starter husband." The lives of many movie stars (our current popular guides as to how a human being should live happily ever after) reveal that they consider marriage vows so easily broken that no one seems to take them seriously. They appear to regard a better measure of commitment as having a child together and cooperating in its upbringing. Agreeing to share amicably in the loving and raising of a child is a form of a vow. When the future happiness of a third person is at stake, people may be willing to work to keep that vow even when they do not want to or cannot live together.

Once a group of elementary school kids came to my eighty-four-year-old widowed mother's retirement home to take oral histories from the elderly residents. The three girls interviewing her asked how long she'd been married. "Fifty years," she said. "To the same person!" they asked, incredulous.

Soon after that I spent some time interviewing her about her life. When my grandparents had died, I had realized that when your older relatives pass away, all the history they hold in their memory dies with them and can never be retrieved. I wanted to capture some of my mother's history for her grandchildren. My mother told me something I did not know. She said that when she and my father were in their twenties, they began to talk about getting married. They decided that a two-person team could accomplish more to benefit the world than two separate individuals. They picked two areas to work on together, race relations and international relations. That explained a lot about our family life!

When I was two, my father took his first teaching job at Talladega College, a traditionally all-black institution, a bold move for a couple raised in Missouri and Tennessee. The Ku Klux Klan burned crosses on the lawn of the minister who lived across the street from us. My father participated in the first sit-in protesting discrimination at a restaurant in the South. When I was five, we moved north, to upstate New York, where our family regularly hosted students from around the world. When I was thirteen, we moved to Korea, where my father helped establish a library school at a university that had books in four languages and no classification system. After 9/11 my mother—in her mideighties—called a local mosque and asked to be introduced to a Muslim woman. They became friends. This was her way of working for peace.

I realized that my parents had been an example of a couple *equally yoked*, a term that comes from a team of horses or oxen yoked together and sharing the work of pulling a wagon or plow. If they pull in different directions, the plow stalls or goes catawampus, and there's no progress. Equally yoked means having the same values, direction, and destination. This does not mean that a couple has to have the same religious beliefs, work at the same company, spend all their free time together, or never have arguments. It means fundamental agreement about what is most important in life and the willingness to work together to achieve their common—and individual—goals.

If a woman decides to become a doctor, her husband or partner is in for many years of irregular hours, accumulating debt, and a chronically tired wife. If a man runs for president, his wife must yield what she might wish to do or say, even how she might wish to dress. She must spend years attending the events, speaking the words, and wearing the clothing that the role they share requires. Zen teacher Norman Fischer has said:

> In relationship, as in spiritual practice, commitment is crucial. In both Zen and marriage there's the practice of vowing, intentionally taking on a path, even if we know we won't get to the destination. Vowing is liberation from whim and weakness. It creates possibilities that would not occur otherwise, because when you are willing to stick to something, come what may, even if from time to time you don't feel like sticking to it, a magic arises, and you find yourself feeling and doing things you did not know you were capable of.[1]

The vows exchanged in a committed relationship help hold us together when we hit the hard parts. If we can hold steady and walk into the hard parts, breathing through our fear that this is the end, humbly accepting help as needed, those hard parts can become the catalyst for greater intimacy and commitment.

What if you have broken a vow, in this case the vow to love and honor someone "as long as ye both shall live"? I suggest that, even if you have divorced, you still love that person. The strength of your original love for him or her may have reversed its polarity, and you may experience it as anger. The aversion, the anger, was perhaps necessary for you to be able to separate, but it is still the energy of love, just turned inside out. It is like a swimmer who reaches the end of a lap and must push off the wall hard in order to turn the forward momentum around and swim off in the opposite direction. If you did not love (and therefore feel anger toward) your partner, you would be able to say with equanimity, "Nice knowing you. Thanks for helping me appreciate jazz music and teaching me how to skydive. See you around." Your separation would be amicable and have no extra energy, positive or negative, no clinging or aversion.

Divorce does not have to mean the end of vows. If the separation was done with a measure of humility and humanity, you can still keep that original love-and-honor vow. You just have to change its means, the ways you carry it out. You won't carry out the love-and-honor vows by living together as a married couple. Instead you could vow never to speak ill of your ex-spouse, especially around your children. You could rejoice in your ex's happiness if he or she remarries or gets a promotion. You could console him when he is ill, be understanding and sympathetic if her next marriage fails or she loses her job, and be compassionate or even help care for your ex when he or she is dying.

What are we actually vowing when we take traditional marriage vows? If we consider the vow "to love," we have to ask, why do we want so much to love and be loved by someone? Loving is a means of merging with another person, physically and psychically. What is the underlying intention behind our desire to merge?

When we are born, we emerge from the One and find ourselves inhabiting separate bodies and minds. This separate existence is a lonely habitation. Our deepest longing is for intimacy, to feel even for a few moments the closing of that sad gap, whether with a person, a pet, or with nature. Love is the only way we humans have to try to get under another's skin, to understand how another being thinks, feels, and approaches life. Our hope in committing to an enduring relationship is to make a deep connection with at least one person, more than one if we have children. We can keep that vow beyond arguments, beyond separation, beyond divorce, beyond death. However, we may have to be creative about how we do it.

One of my personal vows is to support my biological family members. I cannot control how long the marriages of my children will last. But I can do this. When reciting the vow to support my family, I send each one this earnest wish: "May (names of my son, his wife, and their children) have lifelong loving relationships." I also send the phrases of *metta**—loving-kindness practice—to my ex-husband and his new wife. "May you both be free from anxiety and difficulties. May you be at ease and happy together."

The next traditional marriage vow is "to honor" our partner. Again, we need to ask why? What underlies this vow? To honor someone means that we respect him or her. Respect turns out to be a predictor of satisfying and lasting marriages. Drs. John and Julie Gottman from the University of Washington report that they can predict which relationships will not last by observing less than a half hour of a couple's interactions.[2] Disdain, scorn, or contempt, whether expressed in words, facial expressions, or body language, appear to signal a partnership that will not last. Even small expressions of respect and connection, such as looking up from what you are reading when your partner asks a question or comments on something outside the window, is a sign of a relationship that is likely to last.

Respect also infuses us with honest humility. If your partner were superior to you in all aspects of life, would you enjoy being married to him or her? Marriage is an opportunity for both partners to learn about other interesting ways to be in the world, ways that are not natural to their particular personalities. We often observe that people marry their opposite. This is because we are attracted to someone who manifests qualities in the world that we do not. It makes us curious. I have a messy apartment, but it feels nice to be in my lover's clean home! Isn't he adorable, how he organizes his shirts by color and the spices alphabetically in the cupboard? And he, in turn, appreciates the freedom his partner has to just climb out of her clothes and leave them where they lie—until the honeymoon period is over. The formerly cute habits become annoying. "Uptight" replaces "orderly," and "slob" replaces "free spirit" when describing our partner, as respect turns to ridicule and contempt. Contempt is a powerful predictor of a relationship that will not last. Humility means that we realize that our way is only one way, not *the* way, to be in the world. It means that we take our partner on consciously as a teacher.

Now, that's an interesting practice, to take your partner as your teacher. Every time he or she does something that irritates you, you ask, "What is this teaching me about a different way to be in the world? Can I experiment with his or her way instead of mine?"

"In sickness and in health" is a vow of loyalty. It includes not just physical illness, but changes such as depression, losing a job, and dementia. A friend decided to put her husband in a residential "memory unit." This was a difficult decision, but it was in keeping with her marriage vows to love and honor him, because Alzheimer's disease made him ask incessant repetitive questions and insist on being inches away from her all day. It had unraveled her ability to express the sixty years of love she had shared with him. When she could visit him for hours a day and still get her own work done, it became easy for her to show her deep affection for him again.

Marriage is a small, individual-sized experience in caring for and honoring another person. Actually, divorce can be the same experience. So can becoming a parent. A committed relationship forces us to enlarge ourselves, to expand our sphere of affection, our willingness to see the best in another person. I believe that we fall in love with one person for this reason—in order to learn how to love another person more than we love ourselves, and ultimately to learn how to love any "other" we encounter. This is easy to say but often hard to do.

EXERCISE

Questions about Marriage and Divorce to Ponder and Discuss

If you are married or have been married, what did you promise the other person? Did you honestly think you would keep those vows forever? If you divorced, has that "breaking of vows" made you reluctant to make other vows or commitments? Could you write one or two "divorce vows," ways to love and honor your ex-partner at a distance? What do you think you could promise in a marriage vow today? (This question is for everyone, married or not.) Is love itself a kind of vow? If so, what are you committing to when you feel love for someone?

CELIBACY

Celibacy is not just a matter of not having sex. It is a way of admiring a person for their humanity, maybe even for their beauty.

—TIMOTHY RADCLIFFE, Dominican friar[3]

A woman told me recently that she would like to take a vow of celibacy for two years. Her father was a narcissistic, angry, and violent man who still wanted his adult children to be tied to him. She had been married once, to an apparently mild-mannered professor, who turned out also to have an anger problem as well as an addiction to pornography. I was concerned that her celibacy vow might be a reactive one, but she had pondered this possibility carefully for several months. She felt that celibacy would help free her of a pervasive and lifelong belief that for her life to be meaningful and worthwhile, she must be attached to a man. During periods of quiet reflection, she became aware of how her relationships had been off-kilter in a fundamental way and of the suffering these relationships had created.

She felt that a period of celibacy would keep her from starting down the familiar path of seeking yet another potentially troubled relationship. She had always felt lonely when not partnered with someone. During a meditation retreat that involved many periods of sitting out of doors in the meadows and forest around the monastery, she had a deep experience of interconnection with the multitude of beings, people, insects, coyotes, trees, and grasses that surrounded her. She realized that she was never alone.

She wanted to take a vow of celibacy in order to further examine her very old and pervasive feelings of being alone. She had an intuition that by not running away, by walking straight into those feelings, whenever or however they arose, she would emerge into the pervasive and tender companionship that is on the other side.

She was surprised after six months by the experience of a novel feeling of freedom. She felt sheltered and protected by the vow of celibacy. She could interact with men without any part of her mind wondering whether their relationship would become sexual and without her heart feeling conflicted or distressed about that possibility.

Celibacy is different from continence. Being continent means to contain your sexual activity to one relationship, while being celibate means to abstain from sexual activity. A gay man told me about formulating a spontaneous vow of continence, an inner promise not to have sex with anyone besides his partner of twenty-nine years. Although he had been faithful to his partner and had never been promiscuous, he felt moved to make a deeper commitment. He said,

> What was striking was that the very next day, I noticed how differently I regarded people I encountered in everyday situations. It was as though the people around me were officially removed somehow from the category "sexually available," even though I'd never realized before that people even existed in that category. It was a vow I didn't take to be

necessarily a big deal, and that didn't require a change in my behavior, yet making it changed the way I looked at the people around me in a surprising way.

Another young woman who had been involved in many sexual relationships in college came to a meditation retreat and began to question what she had been looking for in these brief encounters. She decided to take a deliberate vow of celibacy for one year. She wrote to tell me that she discovered she turned to sex "when I began to feel awkward in my own skin, or when I felt that something was not quite right in the relationship with a particular man, and sex was a reliable distraction from those uncomfortable feelings." She realized that sex did not promote intimacy for her. Quite the contrary, it was a way of avoiding open communication and tenderness with men.

She used her year of celibacy to develop intimacy with herself, with the workings of her mind and emotions. By stepping back from "actively playing with sexual energy," she was able to examine the phenomenon itself. She explored the difference between sensual desire and sexual feelings, and formulated a new vow to guide her after the celibate year was over.

Whenever I feel myself "needing" something from someone else, rather than trying to get somebody to provide what I need, I will try to find a way to creatively embody and provide/care for that need for myself or others. I will use sensual desire as a reminder to bring that quality of sensual intimacy and gentleness into my awareness itself. I can make love to my visual field with my eyes, or caress the auditory field with my ears, and then allow that experience to become reciprocal.

Sexual desire does not disappear when we take a vow of celibacy. When a group of Western Buddhist teachers asked the Dalai Lama, a lifelong celibate monk, about practicing with sexual feelings, he remarked that it is not something you fight and conquer. Rather, working with desire, whether for food or sex, is a daily practice. A vow of celibacy also helps us to see people not as objects of our desire, but as brothers and sisters, part of the human family that supports our life and path of practice.

I teach a class on sexuality as spiritual practice. One of the most popular speakers is a priest who is a Jesuit novice master. Part of his job is to help men discern whether they have a calling to celibacy. He says that a vow of celibacy must arise naturally. It cannot be tinged with hints of self-hatred, pride, or punishment for sins. It cannot be forced. He says that he has observed that couples must spend a lot of time on keeping a relationship vital and warm. Celibacy gives him the ability to have a deep connection with more than one person, to better serve his students and parishioners. He feels sexual energy arising and folds it into an ongoing investigation of how to use that energy to serve people's spiritual needs.

Susan, the Catholic nun in the section "Vows are Alive, Vows Change," said that celibacy allows her to discover God in other people and in nature and to express her love of God through loving and caring for all creatures. Instead of focusing on a single person, she channels her sexual energy into other forms of intimacy and service for numerous people. It is inspiring to witness her natural, warm-hearted ability to connect with people of all ages and conditions.

EXERCISE

Contemplating Celibacy

If you are so inclined, you can create a vow of celibacy for yourself. First you have to define *celibacy*. Does it exclude all sexual activity? Masturbation? Sexual fantasies? Pornography? Flirting? Undressing people with your eyes? (I know a university professor who realized he had the habit of mentally undressing every attractive woman who walked into his office. He worked diligently and eventually ended this habit. This is a form of a celibacy vow.) If you are married, does your vow exclude all fantasies, flirting, or sexual relationships outside your marriage?

Next you pick a time frame that is realistic, from one month to one year. You might also state what you want to investigate during the time you are celibate. For example you could examine feelings of loneliness, what situations in the past you tried to "solve" with sexual behavior, and how your relationships change when sexual behavior is put aside.

7

PICKED UP AND CARRIED ALONG BY VOWS

ONE VOW CAN GIVE BIRTH TO ANOTHER

Dear brothers and sisters, great people, who brought change, like Martin Luther King and Nelson Mandela, Mother Teresa and Aung San Suu Kyi, once stood here on this stage. I hope the steps that Kailash Satyarthi and I have taken so far and will take on this journey will also bring change—lasting change.

—MALALA YOUSAFZAI, age seventeen,
Nobel Peace Prize lecture, 2014[1]

MALALA YOUSAFZAI, who was shot in the head by the Taliban for her efforts to ensure education for girls in Pakistan, became the youngest recipient of a Nobel Prize. The prize was shared with Kailash Satyarthi, an Indian man who gave up his career as an engineer in order to rescue and rehabilitate thousands of children from forced labor and sexual slavery. Both recipients referred to the "great people" whose lives and vows had inspired them.

The Nobel Prize itself emerged from a reactive vow. Alfred Nobel, who invented dynamite and other explosives, was a pacifist.

Dismayed at being characterized as the man "who became rich by finding ways to kill more people faster than ever before,"[2] he stipulated that his estate would fund prizes for preeminent work in science, medicine, literature, and the furtherance of world peace. The biographies of Nobel laureates are rich in vows and how their vows were inspired by the vows of others. For example, Yousafzai and Satyarthi were inspired by Martin Luther King, who was inspired by Gandhi. Gandhi was inspired by Tolstoy, Jesus, Muhammad, and the Buddha. The chain of vows birthed from previous vows stretches back further than imagination can reach.

Habitat for Humanity is another example. Habitat was formed in 1976 from a vision of "a world where everyone has a decent place to live." Their mission statement reveals their primary vow, "to put God's love into action," followed by a statement about the means: "Habitat for Humanity brings people together to build homes, communities and hope."[3] Habitat has used volunteer labor to build more than five hundred thousand low-cost homes for 1.75 million people in one hundred countries on five continents. The homes they build are seen as a foundation for "breaking the cycle of poverty," another statement that reveals an underlying vow.

Habitat for Humanity was born out of the workings of previous vows made by two couples in 1942 in Americus, Georgia. They wanted to create a "demonstration plot for the Kingdom of God," which ultimately manifested as a farm called Koinonia,[4] from the Greek word for "communion" or "joint effort." Koinonia members based their principles on the New Testament, committing to several principles:

1. Treat all human beings with dignity and justice.
2. Choose love over violence.
3. Share all possessions and live simply.
4. Be stewards of the land and its natural resources.

As an interracial community in the segregated Deep South, Koinonia was subject to intimidation, threats, and terrorist attacks, yet they always responded with nonviolence. The community began constructing modest houses, sold with no-interest mortgages to neighbors living in shacks, a project that birthed Habitat for Humanity. Over sixty years Koinonia has founded many "ministries" (what we would call "means" to carry out their vows), including racial reconciliation, sustainable agriculture, and work with the elderly, refugees, and prisoners and their families.

At times the energy of a strong vow can seem to die out, but it may just go underground, sometimes for centuries. We have two examples in the history of Japanese Zen.

Dōgen Zenji[5] was a Japanese Zen master of the thirteenth century. Within a few generations following his death in 1252, he became virtually unknown except to a small number of Japanese scholars and priests. His writings were rediscovered after nearly seven hundred years and are now studied widely and considered among the best of the world's spiritual literature. Interest in Dōgen's writing helped foster the introduction of Zen into Western countries in the twentieth century. He would probably be surprised to find that now he is regarded as the founder of Sōtō Zen, the largest branch of Zen in Japan, Europe, and America.

Hakuin Zenji,[6] a seventeenth-century Zen master, is credited with reviving Zen practice in Japan at a time when it was stagnant and in its death throes. His religious vocation began when he was a child, as a reactive vow. Terrified by a vivid sermon on the torments of hell, he decided the only way to escape was to become a monk, and he ordained at age fifteen. Although Zen had become stagnant and weighted down with bureaucracy in Japan, Hakuin was inspired by the stories of the deep dedication and enlightenment experiences of the ancient Zen masters in China. Convinced that thoroughgoing awakening was possible, he practiced with great determination for twenty-six years. He told of having many enlightenment experiences, many small openings and some profound insights. Resolving to help others experience the freedom of awakening, he spent the next forty-one years traveling and teaching; he was especially renowned for writing in the vernacular and painting "visual sermons" for laypeople, who were often illiterate. His strong vows caused a rebirth of Zen in Japan, through his emphasis on disciplined training, zazen, and active koan practice. Hundreds of monks came to study with him, and he authorized over eighty disciples to teach. All modern Rinzai masters trace their lineage to Master Hakuin.

When we make a vow, we cannot know if it will become a small but enduring flame that will kindle another's vows, even centuries after we die. We can only do our best to live our vow now.

LIT FROM WITHIN BY VOWS

I don't know Who—or what—put the question. I don't know when it was put. I don't even remember answering. But at some moment I did answer Yes to Someone—or Something—and from that hour I was certain that existence is meaningful and that, therefore, my life, in self-surrender, had a goal.

—DAG HAMMARSKJÖLD, second secretary general
of the United Nations[7]

There are many ways people find their direction in life. Some are inspired by words spoken by a parent or teacher, and they carry those words as a guiding principle. Others join the life work of a charismatic leader and expand it into new arenas, as Martin Luther King did when he carried Gandhi's principles of nonviolence into peaceful protests against racial discrimination in the American South. Some people feel they have been "guided" by unseen navigators to find the right path, or at least the next step on the path. Others have the experience of the path opening by itself before them. Some people undertake months or years of discernment to discover the underlying mission of their life. Others have their life direction revealed suddenly, by a voice or an inner knowing that seems to be of divine origin. Here are two stories of life vows catalyzed by divine inspiration.

A Young Woman with a Clear Purpose
and a Near-Death Experience

A young woman sat down next to me on an airplane. On a whim, I told her I was writing a book on life vows and asked her if she knew what her life purpose was. To my surprise she had an immediate answer. Alissa related that she had found the underlying purpose of her life eight years previously, at age eighteen. Her family life had been chaotic; her father was an angry alcoholic, and her older sister was her only support. One night her sister began packing; she announced that she couldn't endure any more verbal and physical abuse and was leaving home the next morning. Alissa was overcome by outrage and despair at being left to face the abuse alone. She lay on her bed, shaking her fists at the ceiling, shouting to God, "How could you let this happen to me? If you are there, show yourself to me!"

The next day, as she was driving to work, distraught, her car slid off the road and overturned in a ditch. She remembers leaving her body, circling around the car, thinking, "Oh, that's really bad!" and then realizing, "Oh, that's me in there." Then she blacked out and "went to a very peaceful place." She awoke to find her family and friends gathered in sadness around her hospital bed. She was amazed to see among them several unfamiliar people. Later in life she recognized them immediately when they entered her life in beneficial ways.Her family was grieving because they had been told she might not live. Her awakening and rapid recovery were considered a miracle.

Alissa felt that God had given her the message she had so angrily demanded. This was a turning point in her life, the realization that "God loved me as I was, had a purpose for me, and was active in my life." Two years before, she had been at youth camp, "worshiping and hanging out at the altar." The youth leader asked that they all take some time to become quiet inside and then to ask God the purpose of their life. Alissa had a vision of herself standing in front of a large crowd of junior high and high school kids, talking to them about the positive outcome of the most difficult aspects of her life. She knew that her life mission was youth ministry. Somehow she had drifted away from this realization until the vivid intervention of her sister's abrupt departure and her near-death experience.

Alissa told me she was preparing for her calling by taking classes to become a credentialed counselor (which she said would be reassuring to parents of the youth she was guiding) but also by working as a bartender! She recalled being the one person at high school parties who did not drink (a reactive vow to her father's alcoholism), and thus she kept her friends "from dying of alcohol poisoning or falling into the fire." She had decided that parties were a waste of time and then realized "I could get *paid* to clean up other people's vomit."

She explained that when young people discovered that she, a youth pastor who did not drink, worked in a bar, it gave her street credentials and also kept her "anchored in the real world." Her boss would not allow her to talk about religion with customers in the bar, unless the customers initiated the conversation. She found that "there are no walls up in a bar" and that many of her customers were plagued by questions about whether their lives had a purpose and whether a divine force could exist in, let alone create, a world of human cruelty and betrayal.

Prayer for her is a daily and ordinary conversation. She speaks out loud, as though to a friend, and God answers inwardly. She enjoys her chosen work and has realized that her entire life prepared her for helping young people, especially those from chaotic homes. She sees that she is imperfect but not, as she previously believed, broken. She said her two siblings are unhappy precisely because they have not found their life purpose.

Buckminster Fuller: A Life Transformed

In 1927, when he was in his early thirties, Buckminster Fuller was walking along the shores of Lake Michigan, mentally preparing himself to swim out until he was exhausted and drown, so his family could collect life insurance. His young daughter had died, his company had failed, and his family had no savings. Suddenly he found himself suspended several feet above the ground, enclosed in a sphere of white light. A voice said to him, "From now on you need never await temporal attestation to your thought. You think the truth. You do not have the right to eliminate yourself. You do not belong to you. You belong to Universe. Your significance will remain forever obscure to you, but you may assume that you are fulfilling your role if you apply yourself to converting your experiences to the highest advantage of others."[8]

Fuller said this experience infused clear direction and purpose into his life. He spent nearly two years in silent meditation and study, emerging with a vow to "make the world work." He decided to become "Guinea Pig B," the subject in his own lifelong experiment, to determine what a single individual without money or a college degree could contribute to changing the world and benefiting all humanity.

He became one of the first futurists and global thinkers, coining the term *Spaceship Earth* and proposing ways to feed, shelter, and provide renewable energy to the entire population of the world. He was an inventor with dozens of patents and the architect who popularized the geodesic dome. He taught at several universities, wrote twenty-eight books that cumulatively sold over a million copies, and was awarded over fifty honorary doctorates and a hundred awards, including the Presidential Medal of Freedom. He advised, "The minute you choose to do what you really want to do, it's a different kind of life."[9]

Mother Teresa: A Life Rich in Vows

Mother Teresa's life was composed of vows. As you read her story, you encounter vows of every kind—primary, inherited, inspired, religious, binding, reactive, and secret. She was born in Albania and raised by a devout Catholic mother. Her mother, a widow, often invited the city's poor to eat with the family. She told her daughter, "My child, never eat a single mouthful unless you share it with others." When Teresa asked who the dinner guests were, her mother replied, "Some of them are our relatives, but all of them are our people."[10] Teresa's later vocation seems to have been founded upon this inherited vow to see and serve the poor, as if they were family.

Mother Teresa recounted, "From childhood the Heart of Jesus has been my first love. Since the age of five when I first received him, the love for souls has been within. It grew with the years until I came to India to save as many immortal souls as possible from the darkness of unbelief." Thus her primary vow was to love and save souls.

As a teenager, on one of many pilgrimages to pray to the Black Madonna of Letnice, she heard a voice saying, "Follow God . . . serve others," and she made a decision to become a nun. Fascinated by stories of missionaries based in India, she made an inspired vow to teach there. She learned English, the language of instruction in India, and eventually became fluent in Bengali and Hindi as well. At age nineteen she arrived in India and began teaching at a convent school for girls, a career that lasted for twenty years.

She took her first formal religious vows as a nun at age twenty-one, followed by solemn vows at age twenty-seven, promising to live a life of poverty, chastity, and obedience, and to devote herself with particular care to the instruction of youth.

Hidden underneath Mother Teresa's vow to save souls was another, *secret vow*. At age thirty-two, she made what she called a binding vow, revealed only to her spiritual advisor. It was "to return God's unconditional love by giving to God without reservation, anything He asked." She reframed this in several ways over the years, as "Not to refuse Him anything" and "To say yes in all circumstances."

Mother Teresa was increasingly disturbed by the poverty surrounding her in Calcutta. In 1943 there were cyclones, tsunamis, and flooding, resulting in the great Bengali famine, in which 1.5

to 4 million people died, approximately 1 in 15 people. Three years later, Hindu-Muslim violence erupted, and within seventy-two hours at least 5,000 people were killed and 100,000 people left homeless in Calcutta. Vultures feasted on the piled-up corpses.

One month after the riots, Teresa was traveling by train from Calcutta to Darjeeling for her annual retreat. She suddenly experienced "the call within the call." She realized she "had to give up the Loreto convent where I was very happy and go out into the streets to serve the poorest of the poor." She began to hear the voice of Jesus all day, every day, saying, "Come, come, carry me into the holes of the poor. Come, be my light." This divinely inspired vow became the heart of her passionate fifty-year mission to serve the poorest of the poor. It may also have had elements of a reactive vow, a response to the terrible human suffering that impinged upon her heart every waking hour in Calcutta.

She wanted to act immediately but, because she had taken a vow of obedience, she had to receive the approval of her superiors, in particular, the Jesuit archbishop of Calcutta. Her spiritual director, testing whether her vow came from God, ordered her not to think or speak about the call for three months. The archbishop told her to "drop these ideas for all eternity (and) . . . to live in the present and be a perfect nun." Unable to comply, she wrote numerous fervent letters, saying that Jesus was "complaining" to her about delays. Finally, almost two years after her call, the archbishop gave her permission to go ahead.

Mother Teresa took off her nun's habit, put on a plain sari, and left her order, a very painful separation. She spent several months taking basic medical training at a mission hospital. Then she went out alone into the slums of Calcutta with only five rupees in her pocket, trusting in divine Providence. She began by offering water and prayers to those who lay dying on the streets. She started an open-air school for street children and found a building where she could bring sick people for shelter and simple care. Within a year thirteen young Indian women had joined her work and asked to become sisters.

As Mother Teresa carried out her call within a call, many others were inspired to join in her new order, the Missionaries of Charity. In addition to the traditional three vows (absolute poverty, angelic chastity, and cheerful obedience), they promised to give "wholehearted and free service to the poorest of the poor." Thus, over fifty years the personal vow of one tiny but determined woman grew into a great vow, embodied by over 4,500 sisters and 450 brothers, active in 610 missions in 133 countries, including hospices and homes for people with HIV/AIDS, leprosy, tuberculosis, and disabilities; soup kitchens; children's and family counseling programs; orphanages; and schools.

Mother Teresa also established an ingenious way for her vow to be taken up by laypeople who could not ordain because of poor health or family responsibilities. She paired each of them with a sister and asked them to pray for the work that God was doing through that sister. If they were ill or in pain, she asked them to rejoice in their suffering as a way to take on the suffering of those who were poor and dying in Calcutta. It also would bring them into unity with the suffering of Jesus on the cross.

At the age of seventy-three, Mother Teresa had a first heart attack. After her second, a pacemaker was installed, but she kept on working for fourteen more years, keeping a busy schedule until age eighty-seven, when she died during a blackout in Calcutta. What was not known until after her death is that Mother Teresa did all of this despite an ongoing and terrible inner suffering. Soon after she began her mission among the poor, the inner voice of God, her constant companion supporting and guiding her for years, suddenly disappeared. For forty-five years she experienced what she described as severe inner pain and darkness. While she was helping those who had been abandoned and were alone, she herself felt completely abandoned and rejected by God. She faced the greatest test of her vow. Could she continue to carry out her promise without the sustenance she most longed for?

Her private agony became known when her diaries were published after her death.[11] Why would God abandon her when she was so faithfully carrying out his commands? The only time she felt God's presence was when she was immersed in intimate work with the poor and dying. Finally a spiritual counselor helped her understand that when we are fused with the great mystery that some call "God," there is no dialogue because there is no other. As we are able to get out of the way, "it" is able to work through/within us unhindered. We simply act in unison, like the right and left hands helping someone who has fallen down. We don't think about which hand does what part. They work with one perfectly coordinated movement. This is what we call in Zen experiencing our Original Pure Nature.

Following a vow requires sacrifice. We never know what we will have to give up—perhaps everything we cling to. In her last ten years, Mother Teresa came to accept and finally to treasure the darkness as a gift from God, and her suffering at his apparent absence as something that bound her to all those who suffered.

We may think that when we are following divine inspiration, doors will open for us automatically. We have to remember that the divine acts *through* us, through our very eyes, mouth, arms, and legs, through the discernment of our minds, the kindness in our hearts, and the determination of our whole being. Inspiration that does not impel action is of no use. Sometimes the divine shows us where to go, not by illuminating a path, but by firmly closing doors behind us.

The Quaker author and activist Parker Palmer writes about approaching middle age with no clear vocation. He had been waiting for God's direction, in accord with the Quaker counsel "Have faith and the way will open." Frustrated, he consulted an elder, who said, "I'm a birthright Friend (Quaker), and in sixty-plus years of living, the way has never opened in front of me." Seeing Palmer's expression of dismay, she added, "But a lot of the way has closed behind me, and that's had the same guiding effect." Palmer suddenly realized, "There is as much guidance in what does not and cannot happen in my life as there is in what can and does—maybe more."[12]

There are many ways to find and follow our life purpose. Prophets, saints, and evangelists may follow an inner call (and broadcast the fact of that call), but there are many other "ordinary" people who hear and heed an inner prompting that they call a "higher power." They may be followers of any religion or none. They could be carrying out their vow in any kind of job. They might sit down next to you on a bus or airplane. You wouldn't know about their vow unless you ask. The next exercise is a meditation that provides a higher, broader, more objective perspective on our life and may provide clues about its purpose.

EXERCISE

Seeing with the Eyes of God

(Note: It is easier to do this exercise if you keep your eyes closed and hear, rather than read, the instructions. You can have a friend read it to you or record it in your own voice and play it back while you listen.)

Sit quietly in a comfortable position. Close your eyes. Become aware of your breathing, in the places in your body where the sensations of breathing are most vivid. Remain aware of your breathing for a few minutes, letting your mind settle and relax.

Now use the creative power of imagination to lift your awareness up into the sky, where you can look down with the eyes of God (or an angel or an eagle) and see a tiny person who has your name. You watch this person as he or she goes about his or her daily busyness, getting up, going to work or school, doing chores, talking with other people, going to bed at night. Watch the life of this tiny person who has your name for a few minutes.

Questions

- How do you feel about this person?
- If you could whisper a few words of advice to this person, what would you say?

- If you could tell this person his or her life purpose, what would you say?
- If you could give one nonmaterial gift to help this person accomplish his or her life purpose, what would it be?

IMPOSSIBLE VOWS

Beings are numberless, I vow to save them.
Delusions are inexhaustible, I vow to end them.
Dharma gates are boundless, I vow to enter them.
The Enlightened Way is unsurpassable, I vow to become it.

This is a chant that is recited every day at most Zen temples the world over. When you first read these vows, you might be puzzled. They are written in the language of the impossible. They *admit* they are impossible, using words like *numberless, inexhaustible, boundless,* and *unsurpassable.* How can we vow to accomplish what we know to be impossible?

This is a serious question. Should we only take on vows we know we will be able to accomplish and then be able to cross off our to-do list with a smile of satisfaction? Or could we dare to vow an impossible vow?

As we ponder taking on an impossible vow, it is comforting to know that vows can go on for lifetimes and can be picked up by others. The editor in chief of the company that will publish this book was not the first chief editor in the publishing house nor, if he does his job, does he expect to be the last. The company's mission will continue on, embodied in the changing forms, peculiarities, and preferences of its inevitably temporary personnel. A university professor trusts that the hard work of his professional lifetime will be picked up by others and carried on after he retires or dies. The university will morph, but it will continue to educate and train students.

Here are some vows you might think are impossible.

To Found a University to Last One Thousand Years

The oldest continuously operating university in the world, the University of al-Karaouine in Morocco, was founded in 859 by a woman, Fatima al-Fihri. When she decided to use her paternal inheritance for this charitable purpose, did she expect that the benefit of her vow would continue, passed from person to person, for over a thousand years? Probably not. None of us can know how our vows may unfold throughout space and time.

To Found a Temple to Last One Thousand Years

When we founded our monastery, our Zen teacher told us to plan for it to last a thousand years. This is the way a temple-founding vow works in Japan. In America anything over fifty years old is considered "ancient." In Japan there are many temples that are more than one thousand years old. Over the centuries they have burned or tumbled down in earthquakes and been rebuilt many times. It is awe inspiring to walk into their cool, dark depths and feel the presence of a vow that has been passed down through the patient labor of generation after generation of priests, parishioners, and craftspeople. To stretch our awareness as wide as a thousand years reminds us to keep a broad and flexible view as we work with the small pesky issues that inevitably arise day to day in a community of twenty different people working and living together. An impossible vow reminds us to expand our perspective.

To Rescue a Forest Ten Square Feet at a Time

An impossible vow doesn't have to be enacted on a large scale or find its way into history books. I heard a story on national radio[13] about Kevin, a high school teacher who rises before dawn each morning to go to a nearby park where he spends thirty minutes tackling an obstinate problem, rampant English ivy. Kevin was inspired when a guest speaker in his classroom spoke about the problem of invasive

plants. He said to himself, "I need to use some of my time to give service to the forest that I love and to [give] back a little bit [to] the native plants and the native birds." He works in the dark by the light of a head lamp and begins by asking the ivy for forgiveness. He says, "Thank you, ivy, for your tenaciousness, your strength. I ask you to let me take you out for the benefit of the world here."

Although he can only clear ten square feet a day, and the problem seems intractable, Kevin is also inspired by seeing native plants and birds returning to the park. He remembers a children's story about a little boy and his father who discover hundreds of starfish washed up on a beach. When the boy throws one starfish back in the ocean, the father comments that this can't help, as there are too many starfish. The boy replies, "Well, it helped that one."

The ranger for the park observed that it could take decades, or even a century, to pull out all the ivy in the park where Kevin works. She said, "It can be overwhelming when you look at it overall," but adds, "the battle is winnable [if] you set your sights on smaller plots and saving individual trees."[13] Indeed, the No Ivy League of Oregon reports that over a twenty-year span, its volunteers have removed ivy from 103 acres at eighteen hundred sites and saved the lives of over seventeen thousand trees.[14]

To Bring the World to Lasting Peace

Ten years ago I realized that one of my vows was impossible. I had been planning a pilgrimage for peace to Nagasaki, the second city destroyed in Japan by the atomic bomb. I had inherited the vow to work for world peace from my parents, who were dedicated pacifists, not a popular stance during World War II. In junior high we visited the newly built home of the United Nations in New York. World peace seemed possible. I had marched to end the war in Vietnam, and it had ended. Peace seemed possible. But now, at age sixty, I began to ponder the objective likelihood of attaining world peace.

I looked backward over human history and realized that as long as human beings had existed, they had fought with each other, over food, land, partners, or possessions. I meditated on the world, seeing it as if from space, noting areas of conflict as fires blazing up, existing for a time, and then dying back into darkness. As the decades passed, there were recurring areas of flames on all the inhabited continents. I saw innumerable wars over religious differences and many small countries split by civil wars into several even smaller nations, each unable to support itself and thus obligated to attack their former countrymen and neighbors to survive. I looked forward in time and could see no end to this violence and its long-lasting repercussions.

I asked myself, how can I work for world peace when I see it to be unattainable? Then I realized that the power of anger, greed, ignorance, and their resulting violence is so strong it is like entropy. If we do not work against it, if we do not work actively for peace, everything will inevitably run downhill, and then peace, even a piece of peace, will be impossible.

Thus, in full realization that it was impossible, I renewed my vow to work for peace. I began at home. The only world I can bring to peace is my own inner world. My motto became "If I am a little more at peace, the entire world is more at peace."

To Clean All the Plastic from the World's Oceans

Young people, not limited by adult notions of "impossible," can surprise us when they set themselves a goal that seem far beyond their youthful capacities. Boyan Slat is a teenager from Holland. While diving in Greece, he encountered more plastic bags than fish and became interested in how the huge amount of plastic in the earth's oceans could be cleaned up. There are five enormous areas in the world's oceans, called gyres*, that contain billions of tons of concentrated plastic debris. The plastic is ingested by marine organisms and is causing the death of large numbers of fish, birds, and turtles. It also releases toxic chemicals as it degrades. Ideas for removing this huge hazard were very costly, and thus cleanup was deemed impossible until Slat realized that stationary platforms with floating booms could use the oceans currents to harvest the debris passively, and an organization might even sell recycled plastic and operate at a profit. He founded The Ocean Cleanup Project and, at age nineteen, heads an international team of one hundred scientists and engineers that has received $2.2 million in crowdsourced funds in one hundred days.[15]

To Remove Fear from a Diagnosis of Cancer

Taylor Schreiber's first vow was reactive. His beloved grandfather was in the hospital, dying of lung cancer. His uncle was a physician at the same hospital and the family decided that it might be helpful for their kids to see beneficial aspects of medical care by touring the radiology department where the uncle worked. Taylor remembers seeing images of X-rays and ultrasounds, and deciding on the spot to become a doctor. He was ten years old.

Two decades later, Taylor had finished his PhD in the fields of immunology and the biology of cancer. He was halfway through four years of medical school when he realized that he had the symptoms of lymphoma, cancer of the lymph nodes, the heart of the immune system. Ironically, the diagnosis was made on April Fool's Day. As he underwent six months of grueling treatment he gained a humbling perspective that few physicians have, the patient's experience of the treatments doctors routinely prescribe.[16] Current cancer treatments such as chemotherapy essentially poison all the cells in the body, including the immune system, in hopes of killing the fastest-growing cancer cells first. This produces very difficult side effects, debilitating fatigue, baldness, anemia, nausea, constipation, susceptibility to infection, and even the growth of new types of cancer years later.

Taylor made a second vow, to use his particular knowledge and talents to create immunotherapies that harness the body's own natural defenses to kill cancer cells, making cancer treatment less of an ordeal, and thus removing most of the fear and stress that a cancer diagnosis creates. He is now head of research at a company that is creating therapeutic vaccines that will "educate and activate a cancer patient's immune system to recognize and kill cancerous cells."[17]

Can you think of other impossible vows? To ensure that every person in the world has enough to eat? Is safe? Is free from the suffering of disasters, such as fire, flood, earthquake, and war? To offer education and medical care to all the earth's people? What makes a vow impossible? Some vows that seem impossible eventually become reality. For this we have to thank determined people who had strong life missions. A century ago, replacing sick hearts would have seemed an impossible goal, or repairing severed spinal cords or talking through a small box to a person on the other side of the earth or hiding objects in an invisibility field or sending a vehicle ten years and four billion miles into space and landing it on a comet.

Taking up a vow that seems impossible can be, in an odd way, comforting. We don't have to finish the job before we die. It is enough to work on it with sustained diligence as long as we are able and then pass it on to the next generation. Or let them find and tackle an "unsolvable" problem on their own, with the crazy, unquenchable optimism of youth.

EXERCISE

A Thousand-Year Vow

Review vows you have made and consider the possibility that they might be passed on for a thousand years after you die. Does that change how you see your vows or how you would formulate them?

THE BODHISATTVA VOW

For as long as space endures
And for as long as living beings remain
So then may I too abide
To dispel the misery of the world.

—THE DALAI LAMA'S BODHISATTVA VOW[18]

Ordinary people are those who
live being pulled by their karma;
bodhisattvas are those who live
led by their vows.

—OKAMURA ROSHI[19]

There is a particular kind of impossible vow, one that fuels the lives of the people we call saints or, in Buddhism, bodhisattvas. These are people who have dedicated their lives to helping others, often sacrificing their own comfort and even their own health, as they followed a compelling call. They had no intention to become famous or win prizes, but the passion and depth of their call inspired others to join their work so that the vow of a single person became the vow of thousands, a force that spread around the world and lived beyond their life span, reaching out through time to touch us.

Mahatma Gandhi is one of these. He took radical vows of simplicity and of nonviolence in all circumstances and proved their efficacy against the immense wealth and military power of the British Empire. Gandhi once observed, "The best way to find yourself is to lose yourself in the service of others."[20]

I have seen this firsthand. I have known people whose life energy was turned inward, endlessly ruminating on the stories of their own unhappiness, become completely transformed into people whose life energy flowed out in sympathy, kindness, and generosity. The transformation occurred when they recognized someone who was helpless, someone whose suffering was greater than their own. One formerly self-obsessed woman found a place she could love and help others when she began working in a nursing home. She told me, "These old people are so dear! They can't take care of themselves, and I get great satisfaction just helping them with simple things like eating and dressing."

This is the magic of a bodhisattva vow. When the energy of our heart and mind are turned inward, upon the predicament of our own small life and our many small personal unhappinesses, we can sink into depression and even contemplate ending our seemingly pointless and insignificant life. When the energy of our heart and mind turn outward, and we begin to use whatever skills and talents we have to aid others, our life begins to expand toward its true size. We immediately become healthier.

> You will know Life and be acknowledged by it according to your degree of transparency, that is, to vanish as an end and remain purely as a means.[21]

> —DAG HAMMARSKJÖLD

When Mother Teresa was in her eighties, her physical heart began failing, but the determined vow of her spiritual heart kept her working at a daunting pace. Doctors told her she should "slow down." She replied, "I have all eternity to rest and there is still much to do . . . Life is not worth living unless it is lived for others."[22]

We all have this intuition, that our life is not worth living if is devoted solely to feeding, clothing, educating, and entertaining our one body and mind. And yet, these activities can keep us busy until life ends.

Albert Schweitzer advised, "You must give some time to your fellow man." "Even if it's a little thing, do something for those who have need of a man's help, something for which you get no pay but the privilege of doing it."[23]

You get no pay, and you will encounter many difficulties, but selfless work is of its own nature rewarding. Dr. Schweitzer also wrote,

> From the community of suffering I have never tried to withdraw myself. It seemed to me a matter of course that we should all take our share of the burden of pain that lies upon the world.
>
> In my own life, I had times in which anxiety, trouble,

and sorrow were so overwhelming that, had my nerves not been so strong, I might have broken down under the weight. Heavy is the burden of fatigue and responsibility that has lain upon me without break for years. I have not had much of my life for myself. But I have had blessings too: that I am allowed to work in the service of compassion; that my work has been successful; that I receive from other people affection and kindness in abundance; that I have loyal helpers who consider my work as their own; that I enjoy health that allows me to undertake the most exhausting work; that I have a well-balanced temperament, which varies little, and an energy that can be exerted with calm and deliberation; and that I can recognize whatever happiness I feel and accept it as a gift.[24]

On a night flight, I asked the young man sitting next to me in the dark about his life purpose. As others slept around us, he quietly told me he used to be very skilled at playing video games and spent hours a day at it. One day he suddenly realized, "I have developed a tremendous amount of determination, proficiency, and focused concentration, but to what end?" This turning was the birth of his bodhisattva vow. He decided to use his expertise to help others and began a satisfying career helping elderly people move past fear and frustration to learn to use their computers. Later he turned to me, puzzled, and said, "I never talk to people on planes. Why did I talk to you?" This is the power of vows; they touch and move us deeply, freeing us to express and share our heart's aspiration.

People like the Dalai Lama, Gandhi, Mother Teresa, and Dr. Schweitzer are often called saints or bodhisattvas because they devote their lives to selfless service. The word *bodhisattva* is Sanskrit and literally means "enlightenment being." We hear the words "enlightened" and "awakened," but few people talk about what these words mean in actual human experience. To be enlightened is to realize our full potential as human beings, the full potential of our body, mind, and heart.

We would like our body to be healthy, and we do our best to keep it so. People often undertake training, even hiring a personal trainer, in order to enhance the health and capabilities of their body. We would like our mind to be bright and sharp, to be able to see clearly and deeply into any situation and to know intuitively what to do or not to do. In Buddhism we call this capacity of the mind wisdom. We would like our hearts to be open and kind, even with difficult people. We call this capacity of the heart loving-kindness or compassion. People undertake spiritual training, often under the guidance of a teacher, in order to cultivate wisdom and compassion, the health and capabilities of their minds and hearts.

A bodhisattva is a person who has developed these innate capacities to a very high degree, in order to serve others. Bodhisattvas have progressed to the point where they could leave behind their individuality and join with the One great Source of clarity and compassion. (In most religions this is called entering heaven or merging with God. In Buddhism it is called entering nirvana.) However, as they move to do so, they look back and see the immensity of physical and emotional pain in the world. A vow arises spontaneously in their heart, a vow to save everyone who is trapped in the bewildering maze of human suffering and is unable to find their way out by themselves. And they turn back, gladly plunging into their chosen work.

Our monastery is centered around a particular bodhisattva, called Jizo, a figure whose statues can be found all over Japan. Jizo is much beloved there as the guardian of those who need extra help in their life journey. This includes children, women, those who are ill, and those who have passed through the door into what we call death. Jizo has taken a great vow, to not enter nirvana until every last person is saved from suffering. This is an endless vow, a "vow without a wristwatch," as one person put it. Like all great vows, it can only be carried out if we give up wondering when we will get there. Simply carrying out the vow becomes the source of joy.

Because there are so many unhappy beings, and because each one of them will be helped in a different way, Jizo Bodhisattva is able to transform into countless forms, called *division bodies*. In an ancient scripture, Jizo says, "Perhaps I appear in a male body, or that of a woman, or in the body of a god, or dragon, or that of a spirit or ghost. Or I may appear as mountains, forests, streams and springs, as rivers, lakes, fountains or wells, in order to benefit people. Or I may appear in the body of a king, a layman, a prime minister, a monk or nun, in order to teach and rescue beings."[25]

When we take up a vow to help other people and beings, we become a bodhisattva division body. We appear in our particular body, working in our particular realm, giving food and shelter to an abandoned dog, tutoring to a struggling child, a hug to a grieving coworker, meditation instruction to a convict, the shade of a newly planted tree to a hot summer street. Like a parent who feels helpless in the face of a child's pain, we would even be willing to take the pain of others on ourselves if it would relieve them.

Shantideva, a Buddhist mystic of the eighth century in India, spoke poetically of his bodhisattva vow, the impulse to give ourselves away in order to relieve the suffering of others.

> May I become doctor and medicine,
> May I be the nurse for all sick beings in the world, until everyone is healed.
> And during the ages of scarcity, may I change into food and drink!
> May I become an inexhaustible treasure for those who are poor and destitute,
> May I be a protector of those without one, a guide for all travelers on the way.
> May I be a bridge, a boat, and a ship for all who wish to cross the water,

> A bed for those who wish to rest, and a servant to those
> in need.[26]

Despite our desire to help those whose suffering is worse than our own, we cannot always be the strong one, the rescuer. It is important that we also ask for help when we need it, because when we sincerely ask for help, we are the means by which other people can be transformed into bodhisattvas. Bodhisattvas arise in response to true need. We are all in this business together, the business of cocreating bodhisattvas.

It is not enough to live just for ourselves, to pass through life adding only trash to landfills and pollution to the air. The world overflows with troubles, natural and man-made disasters. Every time it seems that human beings are making progress toward a kinder, more intelligent way of being on earth, we seem to slip seriously backward. We hope our life will be able to lessen, even in small measure, the suffering of other beings, not add to it. On dark days, however, we can fall into despair, feeling that our life will be meaningless—a futile effort to gather possessions that our progeny do not want and we cannot take with us after death. We face the truth that everything we have created will fall apart or disappear. Two hundred years hence, who will even be able to identify us in a fading photo?

It is vitally important to remember, however, that two hundred years hence, whatever good we have been able to do in this lifetime will still be moving through the ever-spreading chain of cause and effect, benefiting countless people in ages to come. It is unlikely that we will be there to see these good fruits, so we must formulate and live our vows in the faith that actions and words that arise from clarity and kindness will always bring benefit. As we actualize our vows, we realize that, in order to truly benefit others, we must continue our spiritual practice.

To live guided by vows, to work to benefit others, to ask for help when we need it—these are the best ways to cultivate the clarity that is the intrinsic essence of our minds and to nourish the compassion that is the innate essence of our hearts. These are the best paths to enlightenment for ourselves and also for others.

EXERCISE

Your Bodhisattva Vow

Can you formulate your own bodhisattva vow? And ask for help in carrying it out? "I would like to help heal the suffering of the world by _____. I ask for the help of all the wise and holy beings of past, present, and future to help me carry out this vow." Here are some examples: "I would like to help heal the suffering of the world by giving a home to all homeless people." Or ". . . by feeding everyone who is hungry." Or ". . . by offering myself as a friend to everyone who is lonely."

Appendix 1

Sample Vows

I've made a list of common primary vows. These vows are universal and apply to anyone, anywhere. Each primary vow is followed by actual examples I found in my reading. If a primary vow appeals to you, you can adapt it to fit your life and person. You can then ask yourself, "How will I go about accomplishing this vow? What will be the action I will undertake (the means) to accomplish this vow?" Those means can become subordinate vows.

I VOW TO SEE AND HONOR THE DIVINE IN ALL PEOPLE AND CREATIONS

To seek the face of God in everything, everyone, all the time, and his hand in every happening.

—MOTHER TERESA

To see Jesus in everyone who comes in the door.

—worker at Saint Vincent de Paul

I VOW TO USE MY SKILLS AND TALENTS TO RELIEVE THE SUFFERING OF OTHERS

To exist for the future of others without being suffocated by their present.

—DAG HAMMARSKJÖLD, second secretary general of the United Nations

I wish to give myself unconditionally to the poor lepers. I would gladly give my whole life to them. I am not ashamed to act as mason or carpenter, when it is for the glory of God.

—FATHER DAMIEN, missionary to lepers

What do we live for if it is not to make life less difficult for each other?

—GEORGE ELIOT, nineteenth-century novelist

When I see / the misery / of those in this world / their sadness / becomes mine. Oh that my monk's robe / were wide enough / to gather up all / the suffering people / in this floating world. Nothing makes me / more happy than / the vow / to save everyone.

—Zen master RYOKAN

I VOW TO IMPROVE THE CONDITION OF THE EARTH AND ITS INHABITANTS

To be stewards of the land and all its resources. To treat all human beings with dignity and kindness.

—Koinonia community

I vow to do my best to leave the world better than I found it.

—GEORGE, hospital administrator

To nurture the health of our planet and the people on it for the next seven generations.

—Seventh Generation Company

We pledge ourselves to liberate all our people from the continuing bondage of poverty, deprivation, suffering, gender and other discrimination.

—NELSON MANDELA

To give free access to the sum of human knowledge to every single person on the planet.

—JIMMY WALES, founder of Wikipedia

I VOW TO HELP _____ (A SPECIFIC GROUP OR TYPE OF SUFFERING).

To put an end to all forms of violence against children: slavery, trafficking, child marriages, child labour, sexual abuse, and illiteracy.

—KAILASH SATYARTHI, awarded the 2014 Nobel Peace Prize with Malala Yousafzai

To stay sober and help other alcoholics achieve sobriety.

—"AA Preamble"

To eliminate smallpox and Guinea worm infection in the world.

—DR. RONALD R. HOPKINS, Carter Center, Vice President for Health Programs

My mission is to someday create a free gay India.

—Indian prince SINGH GOHIL, whose family disowned him when he came out as gay

I VOW TO AVOID KILLING AND TO CHERISH ALL FORMS OF LIFE

I am prepared to die, but there is no cause for which I am prepared to kill.

—GANDHI

To choose love over violence.

—Koinonia community

I will treat others as I would like to be treated; and not treat others in a way I would not like to be treated.

—the GOLDEN RULE

What I wish for myself, seek for all people.

—after a saying of MUHAMMAD'S

[Be] tender with the young, compassionate with the aged, sympathetic with the striving and tolerant of the weak and strong, because someday in your life you will have been all of these.

—GEORGE WASHINGTON CARVER,
African American botanist and inventor

SIMPLE VOWS

If only I may grow firmer, simpler, quieter, warmer.

—DAG HAMMARSKJÖLD

[To have] a humble and spontaneous response to Life— with its endless possibilities, and its unique present which never happens twice.

—DAG HAMMARSKJÖLD

MORE ELABORATED VOWS

The ten vows of Tōrei Zenji, a seventeenth-century Zen master:

I vow not to give up in my spiritual quest
I vow not to waver in faith in the dharma
I vow to continue even if in miserable states
I vow to help others
I vow to penetrate all life questions

I vow to give up my body
I vow to refine my functioning in Truth
I vow not to be mean at heart
I vow not to become self-centered
I vow to pass on any understanding

This is a daily prayer, or set of intentions, that a friend recites each morning after meditation:

> God, have mercy on those I love, on those who love me, on those I hate, on those who hate me, on those I'm indifferent toward, and on those who are indifferent toward me.
>
> May I learn to regard everyone with kindness.
>
> If, when hatred or anger arises, they cannot be transformed into kindness, may I be grateful for seeing their arising.
>
> May I meet every moment with attention; whenever I awaken from inattention, may I be grateful for that moment of awakening.
>
> May I be diligent and conscientious in my work.
>
> May I recognize thoughts of greed, desire, hatred, and aversion when they arise, and may seeing them to be thoughts diminish their power over me.
>
> May I be grateful when I perceive elements of my ignorance, and may such moments remind me that there is much more ignorance to be revealed, and may I behave accordingly.
>
> May I be honest and forthright with all people.
>
> May I never regard any fellow being as an enemy; may I be able to understand the lack of distinction between any of us.
>
> May I recognize the spirit of sarcasm whenever it arises and abandon it.
>
> May I rejoice in the good fortune of others.

May my impatience be transformed into patience.
May my resentments be transformed into equanimity.
May I learn generosity. May my stinginess and clinging
    be transformed into generosity.
May I be supportive and loving toward [my partner], and
    may I always strive to listen to what he [or she] says.
May the consolation of [my partner's] love go beyond our
    relationship to bless others and include them.
May I learn to prefer others' good over my own.
May I set myself on the path that leads toward sacrificing
    myself for others, and may I recognize and be grateful
    for others' sacrifices on my behalf.

MY OWN VOWS

Here is the current form of my own vows. For years I have begun
each day with a silent recitation of my own vows and a request for
assistance from the enlightened ancestors and all wise and holy beings. I have found that this practice keeps my energy focused and
helps bring forward, often in mysterious ways, the resources I need
to be effective. I chant the Jizo mantra* at least three times and
then say:

Jizo Bodhisattva, king of vows, please help me to clarify
    and accomplish my deepest life vows.
My first vow is to become fully enlightened, no matter
    how long this takes. I vow never to turn back from
    the path to enlightenment.
My second vow is to help others to reveal their own
    enlightenment. May _____ (fill in names)_____
    become enlightened even before I do.
My third vow is to establish Great Vow Zen Monastery as
    a place of peace, beauty, spiritual renewal, and ever
    deepening practice, for many generations to come.
My fourth vow is to establish Heart of Wisdom Zen

Temple as a place of refuge in the city, a home, a
hearth and a bridge for all in need, for many generations to come.

My fifth vow is to raise at least several clear, strong students who will continue to give the gift of dharma
for many generations to come.

My sixth vow is to write two to seven more books to
support others in their spiritual life and practice.

My seventh vow is to support my dharma family and my
biological family, to help them reach their highest
potentials for happiness and for benefiting others
in their lifetimes.

After I say my vows, I ask for help: "All buddhas and bodhisattvas, all wise and holy ones, all guardian spirits, all spirits of earth,
fire, water, and air, all devas, I ask for your help in carrying out these
vows. Although it may frighten me at times, I am willing to give up
whatever must be given up in order to carry out these vows."

Appendix 2

A Personal Ceremony of Vows

If you do not have a spiritual setting or group in which to make your vows, here are suggestions for doing a ceremony on your own.

- Make the process important: set up an altar, a special place, a shelf, a cabinet top, a corner. You can use photos or images that are meaningful to you. You can add a candle, flowers, or other offerings. Place some paper and a pen on the altar.
- Sit quietly; settle yourself; bring your awareness to your breath.
- After you have done the exercises in this book and feel ready to frame your vows, write out your vows by hand.
- Use positive statements, such as, "I will sincerely undertake to . . .," "I shall . . .," "It is my intention to . . .," or "I vow to . . ."
- Place the paper with your written vows on your altar.
- Wait a few days and return to sit quietly. Reread your vows.
- Do they need simplifying? Clarifying?
- Make a beautiful copy of your vows, using any media.
- If you can, ask three people (together or singly) to hear you read your vows. Ask for their support. If this is too intimate, go to three places that might be affected by your vows and speak them out loud.
- Place your vows on your altar.
- Light a candle, say a prayer, or do a chant; ring a bell and read your vows out loud.

- Ask for help for any positive source. (For example, "I humbly ask for the support of all wise and holy beings, past, present, and future, in helping me to accomplish these vows.")
- Say your vows from your heart each day for one hundred days. Do this even if you feel like you have failed or your vows have been muddied.

Notes

INTRODUCTION

1. Shohaku Okamura, *Living by Vow,* ed. David Ellison (Somerville, MA: Wisdom Publications, 2012).
2. Vineet Khare, "Arunima Sinha: Indian is first woman amputee to climb Everest," *BBC: News India,* June 11, 2013, www.bbc.com/news/world-asia-india-22751294.
3. Marisha Wojciechowska-Shibuya, "A boy's childhood dream brings water to 500,000 people." *Maxim News Network,* April 18, 2008, text available at https://plus.google.com/photos/107993027105954241749/albums/6051858564700932801.
4. "Malian Muslim hailed for saving lives at Paris market," *France24,* January 12, 2015, www.france24.com/en/20150112-muslim-hailed-saving-lives-paris-kosher-store-Lassana-Bathily.
5. Kazuaki Tanahashi, *Endless Vow: The Zen Path of Soen Nakagawa* (Boston: Shambhala Publications, 1996).
6. Robert J. Lifton, *The Nazi Doctors: Medical Killing and the Psychology of Genocide* (New York: Basic Books, 1998).
7. Dan Buettner, *New York Times Magazine,* October 24, 2012, www.nytimes.com/2012/10/28/magazine/the-island-where-people-forget-to-die.html.

CHAPTER 1: ABOUT VOWS

1. Andrew Carnegie, *The Gospel of Wealth and Other Timely Essays* (New York: The Century Company, 1901), 22.

2. Agnes de Mille, *The Life and Work of Martha Graham* (New York: Random House, 1991), 264.

3. Ben Carson, National Prayer Breakfast Speech (transcript), February 7, 2013, www.freerepublic.com/focus/f-bloggers/2986815/posts.

4. Mohandas K. Gandhi, *The Collected Works of Mahatma Gandhi*, vol. 25 (New Delhi, India: Ministry of Information and Broadcasting, Publications Division, 1960), 558.

5. Mohandas K. Gandhi, quoted in "Epigrams from Gandhiji," www.mahatma.com/php/showNews.php?newsid=59&linkid=11.

CHAPTER 2: DIFFERENT KINDS OF VOWS

1. *Albert Schweitzer Biography*, The Biography Channel, www.thebiographychannel.co.uk/biographies/albert-schweitzer/quotes.html.

2. Albert Schweitzer, *Memoirs of Childhood and Youth*, trans. Kurt Bergel and Alice R. Bergel (Syracuse, NY: Syracuse University Press, 1997), 3–41.

3. Ibid., 29–30.

4. Albert Schweitzer, *Out of My Life and Thought: An Autobiography* (New York: Henry Holt, 1933).

5. Ibid., 103.

6. Ibid., 185.

7. Ibid., 271.

8. Ibid., 268.

9. Charles Bethea, "Remembering a Movement: Mayor Kasim Reed," *Delta Sky* (August 2013), http://deltaskymag.com/Sky-Extras/favorites/Mayor-Kasim-Reed.aspx.

10. Andrew Solomon, *Far from the Tree: Parents, Children and the Search for Identity* (New York: Scribner, 2012), 242–45.

11. Ibid., 207.

12. Jane Goodall, *Reason for Hope* (New York: Warner Books, 2000).

13. Charles Colson, *Born Again* (Grand Rapids, MI: Chosen Books, 1976).

14. Tim Weiner, "Watergate Felon Who Became an Evangelical Leader Dies at 80," *New York Times*, April 22, 2012, www.ny times.com/2012/04/22/us/politics/charles-w-colson-water gate-felon-who-became-evangelical-leader-dies-at-80.html.

15. Jan Chozen Bays, *Jizo Bodhisattva: Guardian of Children, Travelers, and Other Voyagers* (Boston: Shambhala Publications, 2003).

16. Wojciechowska-Shibuya, "A Boy's Childhood Dream."

17. Ibid.

18. Ellen Burstyn, *Lessons in Becoming Myself* (New York: Riverhead Books, 2006).

19. Vincent A. Smith, *Asoka: The Buddhist Emperor of India* (Delhi: Low Price Publications, 1890).

20. S. Dhammika, *The Edicts of King Asoka: An English Rendering* (Kandy, Sri Lanka: Buddhist Publication Society, 1993), www .cs.colostate.edu/~malaiya/ashoka.html.

21. Michael Moss, *Salt Sugar Fat: How the Food Giants Hooked Us* (New York: Random House, 2013), 95–120.

22. Douglas McGrew, "How Carrots Became the New Junk Food," *Fast Company*, March 22, 2011, www.fastcompany.com/1739774/ how-carrots-became-new-junk-food.

23. Aaron Aupperlee, "Huff Post Religion," *Huffington Post*, July 3, 2012, www.huffingtonpost.com/2012/07/03/chris-simpson -former-whit_n_1644824.html.

24. All quotations from TJ Leyden are from this article: "Former Skinhead Tells His Story," Southern Poverty Law Center, www.splcenter.org/get-informed/intelligence-report/browse -all-issues/1998/winter/a-skinheads-story.

CHAPTER 3: HELP IN FORMING VOWS

1. Bruce Newman, *San Jose Mercury News*, April 13, 2013, www .mercurynews.com/bay-area-news/ci_25560201/life-turned -upside-down-by-boston-marathon-bombing.

2. Amanda North's touching reunion with the woman she saved can be seen at "Boston Bombing Victim Reunited with

Her Hero," *CNN: Anderson Cooper 360,* July 4, 2013, http://ac360.blogs.cnn.com/2013/06/04/wednesday-on-ac360-boston-bombing-victim-reunited-with-her-hero/.

3. Lori Weiss, "How One Woman's Bucket List Is Making a World of Difference," *Huffington Post: Marlo Thomas,* September 19, 2012, www.huffingtonpost.com/2012/09/19/marlo-thomas-how-one-womans-bucket-list-is-making-a-world-of-difference_n_1878832.html. All quotes from Terry Huddleston are from this source.

4. Up-to-date career clothing can be donated through www.dressforsuccess.org (clothing for women) and www.careergear.org (for men). A comprehensive site for recycling information and local recycling centers is www.earth911.com. Electronic media (cell phones, cassette tapes, compact discs, floppy disks, jewel cases, videotapes) can be recycled through Alternative Community Training (ACT), 2200 Burlington Street, Columbia, MO 65202, (800) 359-4607, www.actservices.org/recycling.

5. History: Phapama Initiatives 2014, www.phaphama.org/index.php?sid=103.

6. "Missions of Service," Mankind Project, http://mankindproject.org/missions.

7. Jeffrey Abrams, *101 Mission Statements from Top Companies: Plus Guidelines for Writing Your Own Mission Statement* (Berkeley: Ten Speed Press, 2007).

8. Christopher Bart, "Sex, Lies and Mission Statements," *Business Horizons,* November–December 1997, 9–18.

9. Patricia Jones and Larry Kahaner, *Say It and Live It: The Fifty Corporate Mission Statements That Hit the Mark* (New York: Doubleday, 1995).

10. Robert Emmons, *The Psychology of Ultimate Concerns* (New York: Guilford Press, 1999), 103–4.

11. Ibid., 45.

12. Viktor Frankl, *The Doctor and the Soul: From Psychotherapy to*

Logotherapy, trans. Richard and Clara Winston (New York: Vintage Books, 1986), ix–xii.

13. Emmons, 54.
14. Ibid., 92–93.
15. Ibid., 94.
16. Ibid., 109.

CHAPTER 4: MAINTAINING VOWS

1. Benjamin Franklin, *The Autobiography of Benjamin Franklin: In His Own Words, the Life of the Inventor, Philosopher, Satirist, Political Theorist, Statesman, and Diplomat* (ReadaClassic. com, 2010), 146.
2. Ibid., 166.
3. Meredith Lee, "Popular Quotes: Commitment," Goethe Society of North America, March 5, 1998, www.goethesociety .org/pages/quotescom.html.
4. Ajahn Amaro, "English Section: Spiritual Friendship," *Buddha Sasana* September 19, 1993, www.budsas.org/ebud/ebdha028.htm.
5. *US News: NBC News*, October 25, 2005, www.nbcnews .com/id/9809237/ns/us_news-life/t/rosa-parks-matriarch -civil-rights-dies.
6. Mike Dorning, "Rosa Parks Honored with Congressional Gold Medal," *Chicago Tribune*, June 16, 1999. http://articles .chicagotribune.com/1999-06-16/news/9906160104_1_rosa -parks-montgomery-bus-congressional-gold-medal
7. Ryu Sakuma, "Gyogi," in *Shapers of Japanese Buddhism*, ed. Yusen Kashiwahara and Koyu Sonoda (Tokyo: Kosei Publishing Company, 1994), 3–13.
8. www.littledressesforafrica.org/blog.

CHAPTER 5: THE CHALLENGES VOWS PRESENT

1. Viktor Frankl, *The Doctor and the Soul*, trans. Richard and Clara Winton (New York: Vintage, 1986).

2. Yusen Kashiwahara, and Koyu Sonoda, *Shapers of Japanese Buddhism* (Tokyo: Kosei Publishing Company, 1994), 14–25.

3. Viktor Frankl, *Man's Search for Meaning* (New York: Washington Square Press, 1959).

4. Andrew Solomon, *Far from the Tree: Parents, Children and the Search for Identity* (New York: Scribner, 2012), 431–32.

5. Ibid., 445–49.

6. Alan Yentob, "Do or Die: Lang Lang's Story," BBC, Fall 2012, www.bbc.co.uk/programmes/b01nypph.

7. Carl Jung, *Memories, Dreams, Reflections*, ed. Aniela Jaffe, trans. Richard and Clara Winston (New York: Vintage, 1961).

8. David Whyte, "All the True Vows," in *The House of Belonging* (Langley, WA: Many Rivers Press, 1997).

9. Daniel Everett, *Don't Sleep, There are Snakes: Life and Language in the Amazonian Jungle* (London: Profile Books, 2009).

CHAPTER 6: THE VOWS OF RELATIONSHIPS

1. Norman Fischer, "When You Greet Me I Bow," *Shambhala Sun*, September 2011: 44–45.

2. John Gottman, Robert Levenson, and Erica Woodin, "Marriage and Couples Research," April 11, 2010, www.gottman.com/marriage-couples-research/research-abstracts-marriage-couples/.

3. Timothy Radcliff, *Guardian: London*, August 3, 1992, quoted in Robert Andrews, *The Columbia Dictionary of Quotations* (New York: Columbia University Press, 1993), 126.

CHAPTER 7: PICKED UP AND CARRIED ALONG BY VOWS

1. Malala Yousafzai, Nobel Lecture, Oslo, December 10, 2014 www.nobelprize.org/nobel_prizes/peace/laureates/2014/yousafzai-lecture_en.html.

2. Ken Porter and Stephen Wynn, *Lainton in the Great War* (South Yorkshire, England: Pen and Sword Books Ltd, 2014), 30.

3. Habitat for Humanity, www.habitat.org/how/historytext.aspx.

4. Koinonia: History, www.koinoniafarm.org/koinonia-history -timeline.

5. Kazuaki Tanahashi, ed., *Moon in a Dewdrop: Writings of Zen Master Dōgen* (San Francisco: North Point Press, 1985), 3–25.

6. Norman Waddell, trans., *Hakuin's Precious Mirror Cave* (Berkeley, CA: Counterpoint, 2009).

7. Dag Hammarskjöld, *Markings*, trans. Leif Sjoberg and W. H. Auden (New York: Vintage Books, 2006), 108.

8. "About Fuller," Buckminster Fuller Institute, https://bfi.org/ about-fuller/biography.

9. "Biography 1927–1947," *Bucky Fuller Now,* http://www.bucky fullernow.com/sec-3-bio-of-buckminster-fuller-1927---1947 .html.

10. "Blessed Mother Teresa of Calcutta," www.biography.com/ people/mother-teresa-9504160.

11. Brian Kolodiejchuk, *Mother Teresa: Come Be My Light, The Private Writings of the "Saint of Calcutta"* (New York: Doubleday, 2007).

12. Parker Palmer, *Let Your Life Speak: Listening for the Voice of Vocation* (San Francisco: Jossey-Bass, 2000), 38–39.

13. Tom Banse, "A Modern Greek Saga: Sisyphus and the Ivy," *OPB: Earthfix,* January 6, 2014, http://earthfix.opb.org/flora -and-fauna/article/a-modern-greek-saga-sisyphus-and-the-ivy.

14. The City of Portland, *The Ivy Files,* www.portlandoregon.gov/ parks/article/201781#Ivy%20Removal%20Methods.

15. The Ocean Cleanup, www.theoceancleanup.com.

16. "'Ideal M.D./Ph.D. Student' Has Luck On His Side," University of Miami Health Systems, May 1, 2012, http://med.miami .edu/news/ideal-m.d.-ph.d.-student-has-luck-on-his-side.

17. "Heat Biologics, Inc. Appoints Taylor H. Schreiber, M.D., Ph.D. as Vice President of Research and Development," Heat

Biologics, March 5, 2014, www.heatbio.com/news/press-re leases/detail/175/heat-biologics-inc-appoints-taylor-h-sch reiber-m-d.

18. Dalai Lama, "Generating the Mind for Enlightenment," www .dalailama.com/teachings/training-the-mind/generating-the -mind-for-enlightenment. This is the version from our monastery chant book.

19. Shohaku Okamura, *Living by Vow,* ed. David Ellison (Boston: Wisdom Publications, 2012), ix.

20. Mahatma Gandhi, quoted in *Forbes,* www.forbes.com/sites/ ashoka/2012/10/02/12-great-quotes-from-gandhi-on-his-birthday.

21. Dag Hammarskjöld, *Markings,* trans. Leif Sjoberg and W. H. Auden (New York: Vintage Books, 2006), 134.

22. Stan Griffin, "Teresa: Something Beautiful for God," www .workersforjesus.com/teresa.htm.

23. *Albert Schweitzer Biography,* www.thebiographychannel.co.uk /biographies/albert-schweitzer/quotes.html.

24. Schweitzer, *Out of My Life and Thought,* 280–81.

25. Bays, *Jizo Bodhisattva,* 195–99.

26. Shantideva, *A Guide to the Bodhisattva Way of Life* (Dharamshala, India: Library of Tibetan Works and Archives, 1979). This is the version from our monastery chant book.

Glossary

bodhisattva. Literally, "enlightenment being." One who has forgone entry into nirvana (heaven) in order to help those who are still suffering on earth. Bodhisattvas often serve particular needs. Jizo Bodhisattva is the guardian of women, children, those who have died, and travelers, both on the earthly and spiritual planes. Bodhisattvas are similar to a saint in the Western world but are archetypal representations of qualities present in everyone, waiting to be revealed.

dharma. The underlying principles or laws that govern the lives of everything, from individuals to the cosmos. Also, how an individual lives in accord with those laws.

gyre. A large rotating whirlpool of ocean currents where marine plastic collects.

koan. A story, phrase, or question used to point to and also test a Zen student's understanding of the Ultimate. A well-known koan is "What is the sound (of one hand)?"

loving-kindness (*metta* in Sanskrit). A practice of cultivating a fundamental attitude of openhearted benevolence. It is especially helpful when you are feeling negative emotions—irritation, anger—toward someone. One method for doing loving-kindness practice is to say these phrases silently as you breathe out: "May (I/you/they) be free from fear and anxiety." "May I/you/they be at ease." "May (I/you/they) be happy." You begin with yourself, to ease your own distress, and then move to others.

mantra: A word or phrase that is chanted in order to invoke certain qualities in yourself and in the world. For example, the Jizo mantra calls forth benevolence, determination, optimism, fearlessness, and deep vows.

roshi: An honorific literally meaning "old teacher," given to mature Zen teachers in Japan.

sangha. The community of those who follow the teachings of the Buddha. More narrowly, those who are ordained as Buddhist monks and nuns.

torii. A traditional Japanese gate found at the entrance to shrines, marking the boundary between the ordinary and sacred realms.

zazen. Seated silent meditation.

Index